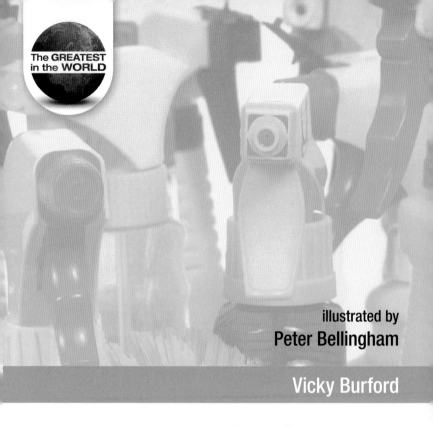

illustrated by
Peter Bellingham

Vicky Burford

The Greatest

Household

Tips in the World

A 'The Greatest in the World' book

www.thegreatestintheworld.com

Illustrations:
Peter Belllingham
www.peterbellinghamillustration.co.uk

Cover & layout design:
the designcouch
www.designcouch.co.uk

Cover images:
© Artovista; © Rene Drouyer; © Kica Henk; © Tom Perkins
all courtesy of www.fotolia.com

Copy editor:
Bronwyn Robertson
www.theartsva.com

Series creator/editor:
Steve Brookes

First edition published in 2006 by Public Eye Publications

ie World Ltd.

duced,
/ any means,
se, without
ony Rossiter
l by him
1988.
il

ritish Library

ISBN 978-1-905151-61-5

Printed and bound in China by 1010 Printing International Ltd.

Contents

A few words from Vicky…

If anyone had told me ten years ago that I would write a book on household tips, I would have laughed for weeks. Me, with my constant pile of dirty dishes in the sink and a rather enormous pile of clothes waiting to be washed in the corner of the bedroom – not a chance! However, the single life is rather different from running a home with children and so when my first daughter came along nearly nine years ago, shortly followed by my second daughter eighteen months later, I realised the importance of keeping on top of the daily chores. Although I thoroughly enjoyed motherhood, I found myself totally overwhelmed by the constant demands of housework … a woman's work is truly never done,

I therefore set myself the task of finding the quickest and most effective ways of doing the chores to enable me more time for my family (and myself) – and I feel that I have succeeded to such a degree I wanted to share my tips with you. Male or female, with or without children, life is too short to spend it doing housework, so take a look inside and give yourself more time to enjoy life.

I have become fascinated by the endless, often unexplainable little tricks for cleaning those seemingly impossible marks away. Although not an eco-warrior, I have become increasingly interested in finding ecologically sound ways to keep my house clean, and I will certainly never look at a tumble dryer fabric sheet, bottle of vinegar, or a can of cola in the same way again!

Many of these time, labour, and money saving tips have been passed on to me over the years by friends and family (a big thank you to Mum and Mum-in-Law for their seemingly never ending supply of advice) and some I have simply developed myself – usually when in a desperate hurry to clean up before a visitor arrives.

I hope you find these tips useful and although I cannot guarantee that they will all work for everyone, they have certainly all come in useful for me at one time or another.

Happy housekeeping!

Vicky

If you can organise your kitchen, you can organise your life.

Louis Parrish

Kitchen

chapter 1

chapter 1
Kitchen

This is usually the most 'well-used' room in the house. All manner of things happen in this room, cooking, entertaining friends, washing, and homework. Because of this it takes a lot more effort than the rest of the house to keep clean and tidy. I have included within this chapter some tips specifically aimed at making many of the chores a little less time-consuming and hopefully save you some money along the way.

Free storage unit

The free cardboard wine carriers usually available from your local supermarket make great storage units for your household cleaning products. They are easy to carry around the house and keep everything neat and tidy under the sink.

Cheap food covers

Shower caps freely available in many hotel bathrooms make really good food covers — and can be washed over and over again. They have an elastic rim which holds them perfectly in place over a plate or bowl and it saves on using cling film.

Old facecloths

When a facecloth becomes very tatty or discoloured, cut off one corner and use the remainder as a household cleaning cloth. (Cutting the corner reminds you that it is not for faces.)

Roasting tins

If you periodically soak your roasting tins for an hour or so in a solution of biological washing powder and warm water, this will remove any existing marks and help to prevent any further stains from sticking. For particularly bad stains, heat the solution in the roasting tin on the hob for about ten minutes to help with their removal.

Wooden chopping board

Whenever you clean your wooden chopping boards or bread boards, sprinkle them with salt and scrub them down before rinsing with fresh water as this will help to restore the wood to its original colour. Be sure to rub in the direction of the wood grain and for an extra clean and bright board, try rubbing the surface of it with a cut lemon to bleach it. Allow the wooden board to dry thoroughly before using it again.

Quick tip

EASY CLEAN MICROWAVE

If you find your microwave difficult to clean, because food has become hardened on, then pop a wedge of lemon into a bowl of water. Put this into the microwave and heat for 3–5 minutes on full power (depending on the power of your microwave); not only will this help to soften the cooked on food, but it will leave your microwave smelling fresh.

Scrambled egg

After preparing scrambled egg, make cleaning the saucepan easier by holding it upside down under cold running water for a few minutes immediately after use.

Sticking rubber gloves

Surprisingly, rubber gloves can be more difficult to remove if you have been using them in hot water as your hands tend to get a bit sweaty and swell slightly. To remove the gloves more easily, first run cold water over them and they will slip off with no trouble.

Kitchen blender

An easy way to clean a food blender after use is to fill the container halfway with hot water and add a couple of drops of washing up liquid or half a teaspoon of dishwasher powder. Cover the blender and turn it on for a few minutes, then rinse with fresh water and dry.

Bacteria-free kitchen

Baby's bottle sterilising fluid (or tablets made up to the recommended formula) is a great anti-bacterial cleaner for around the kitchen. Work surfaces, chopping boards, bread boards, mugs, teapots, and dishes can all be sterilised using this fluid. Afterwards you can use the solution to freshen up your dishcloths, sponges, vegetable brushes etc. and then, finally, when you have finished simply pour the remainder down the sink to keep the drains smelling fresh.

Potato peeler

When an old vegetable peeler becomes blunt it can be brought back to life using a nail file. Just insert the nail file or emery board into the slot in the peeler and rub it along the edge of the cutter.

Refrigerator mildew

If you suffer from a mildew build up inside your refrigerator, this can be prevented if you occasionally wipe down the inside with white vinegar.

Remember, if you ever need to switch off your refrigerator, it is vital that you do not close the door fully, or it will smell very unpleasant next time you come to use it. Hang a dishcloth over the door to prevent it from closing accidentally.

Cooking spills

Whenever you are cooking, keep to hand a dishcloth dampened with clean soapy washing-up water. This enables you to mop up any cooking spills immediately before they become cooked or dried on and difficult to remove.

Shopping list

It is a very good idea to keep a copy of every shopping list you make and be sure to add to it those items you remember in the supermarket. After a few months you can spend a little time combining these lists into one comprehensive list to which you can refer every time you need to do a shop. This acts as a mind jogger, and will prevent you from ever forgetting those bin bags again. You might be surprised how useful you find this tip.

Non-crack glassware

If you rub the outside of a glass or earthenware casserole dish with a raw onion before cooking, then this will prevent the dish from cracking as it is heated.

Quick tip

STUCK GLASSES

Two glasses that are stuck together—one inside the other—can be easily separated without any damage. Stand the bottom glass in hand-hot water and fill the top glass with cold water. The hot water will cause the bottom class to expand, and the cold water will cause the top glass to contract, resulting in them easily coming apart.

Easier defrosting

After defrosting your freezer, dry the inside well and then apply a thin layer of glycerine to all the internal surfaces. When you next defrost the freezer the ice will come away much more easily.

Moving kitchen appliances

If you have to move large kitchen appliances such as refrigerators or cookers to clean behind them then sprinkle some talcum powder on the floor in front of them and they should slide out a lot more easily.

Gleaming sink

If you have a stainless steel sink, and are fed up with it looking mottled and dull, it can be made to really gleam by sprinkling the dry sink surface with a little flour then buffing it up with a soft cloth.

Easy clean oven

After cleaning your oven, rub the inside with a paste made of water and bicarbonate of soda. This will make the oven much easier to clean next time.

Quick tip

GLASS OVEN DOORS
When splatters of food have burnt on to your oven door and are tough to remove, use a disposable razor on the glass to remove the worst before cleaning the residue away.

Plate warming

If you have a large number of guests for dinner, and you need to heat plates but have no room in your oven, try putting them in the dishwasher on a short or drying cycle. The dishwasher keeps them at just the right temperature for a very long time, so if your meal is taking longer than you expected to cook, your plates will not be cooling. An alternative, if you have a dirty load in the dishwasher, is to pop your cold plates in the microwave for a few minutes. It would be best to wet the plates first, with cold water, to avoid the possibility of them cracking.

Ripe fruit

If you find the fruit in your fruit bowl goes bad almost overnight, then make sure that you keep your bananas separate from the rest of the fruit. Bananas release a gas that causes other fruits to ripen far more quickly; so keep your bananas separate from your fruit bowl and you will have solved the problem.

On a positive note however, this can be used to your advantage; if you need to ripen tomatoes, avocados or pears quickly, simply pop them in a brown paper bag with a banana overnight and before you know it you will have lovely ripe fruit.

Dishwash dishcloth

To ensure your dishcloth is always perfectly clean, simply pop it in the top of your dishwasher each time you turn it on. Ensure that you are careful when you remove it, as it will be very hot.

Tight lids

If you don't have one of those fancy jar openers and are having trouble opening tight bottle tops or jar lids, either try removing the top whilst wearing a pair of rubber gloves or put a wide rubber band around the lid, then twist open. Both these methods work really well.

Blunt grater

If your kitchen food grater has become blunt and isn't grating as efficiently as it should, try rubbing the blades with a fine grade sandpaper to improve its grating ability.

Kitchen bin odours

There's nothing worse than the smell of old waste every time you open your kitchen bin. Use the following ideas to help eliminate these odours:

- Sometimes, when you are removing the bin bag, it snags and kitchen waste can leak out into the bin base. Avoid nasty drips on the kitchen floor by always taking the bin outside to change the bag.

- Every time you change the bin put a couple of sheets of old newspaper in the bottom to soak up these drips.

- Try to get into the habit of placing a scented tumble dryer sheet at the bottom of the bin on top of the newspaper whenever you change the refuse bag.

- Periodically wash out the bin with a weak bleach solution.

Odour-free hands

If you have been preparing fish, onion, or garlic dishes and your hands smell, then simply rub your hands over a stainless steel bowl, pan or other kitchen gadget—even the stainless steel taps will do—and the smell should disappear.

Alternatively you could wash your hands with lemon juice, or dampen them and rub with salt, before rinsing under running water.

Stop cracking glass

If you remember to always put a metal spoon into a glass before pouring in any hot liquid, then the metal will absorb the heat quickly which will prevent the glass from cracking.

> My theory on housework is, if the item doesn't multiply, smell, catch fire, or block the refrigerator door, let it be. No one else cares. Why should you?

Emma Bombeck

Food storage

Remember that packet foods such as rice, pasta, pulses, cereals etc. should always be stored in airtight containers or jars. Don't be tempted to leave them in your kitchen cupboard in their original packaging once opened. Even quite tightly closed packets can be easy prey for determined pests which are attracted to the faintest aromas.

Also ensure that any crumbs of food spilt in cupboards are cleared away immediately to avoid bugs. Sweet foods such as sugar, cakes, and biscuits are a special attraction to ants, so always keep these in airtight containers as well.

Pleasant room scent

Often after cooking fish, or some other strong smelling food, I find the odour seems to permeate the entire house for days. If this happens to you, then try the following idea. First of all boil up a pan of water and then add some ground cinnamon and an apple cut in half. If you leave this simmering on the stovetop for a while, it will remove all traces of the unpleasant smell. In fact, this is such an effective room freshener, that you might find yourself using it before guests arrive.

Sharper scissors

I was always throwing away blunt scissors until I discovered this quick and easy way of sharpening them myself. All you need to do is fold a piece of fine grade sandpaper or aluminium cooking foil into four and then cut into the folded piece about half a dozen times. Do this regularly and you will always have sharp scissors in the drawer.

SPAGHETTI MATCHES

If you are trying to light candles or a real fire and you have forgotten to buy those useful long matches or tapers then try using a long piece of dried spaghetti. It works just as well as a taper, it's long enough to reach most places, and if it goes out before you have finished, you have plenty more in the packet.

Plastic bag storage

Everybody I know seems to have a cupboard or drawer filled with plastic supermarket bags that they rarely use. Nowadays, with recycling and re-using being so important, why not take the time to store your plastic bags properly, so that they can be easily accessed when needed? If you fold and store them in empty man-size tissue boxes, when you need a bag you can then pull one out of the box just as you would a tissue.

Fresh thermos

Sometimes your thermos flask can become really smelly, and no amount of washing can remove the unpleasant odour. If this is the case then you can easily refresh it by pouring one tablespoon of vinegar and one level teaspoon of salt into the flask. Pop the lid on securely, then shake well and rinse out thoroughly under running water. As if by magic, the smell has gone.

How to defrost your refrigerator / freezer

- Wait until your stocks of food are low so that you have less food to keep cold.
- Store perishable food in a good friend's fridge or freezer or in cool bags containing ice blocks.
- Switch off your fridge/freezer and open all the doors.
- Place large bowls at the base of the fridge/freezer to catch drips of water and surround the base with old towels, remembering to change these frequently as they become wet.
- To accelerate the process pop a hot water bottle into the worst affected areas and refill as it cools down.
- Once all the ice has gone, thoroughly clean and dry the inside of your fridge/freezer.
- Apply a thin layer of glycerine to all the internal freezer surfaces, which will help the ice to come away more easily next time you need to defrost.
- Wipe down the inside of your fridge with white vinegar which will help to prevent any mildew from forming.
- Turn your fridge/freezer back on and allow it to reach correct temperatures before refilling with food items.

Things to remember

- A freezer runs more efficiently when it is full. Fill empty spaces with bottles of water.
- Keep a small bowl of baking soda or a small piece of charcoal in your fridge to absorb any strong odours.

Scaled kettles

To remove lime scale from inside your kettle you have three options. First you could use white vinegar diluted with water in the ratio of one part white vinegar to ten parts water. Leave this solution in the kettle overnight. Alternatively, you could fill the kettle full of water, add two denture cleaning tablets and leave overnight for the lime scale to dissolve. Finally you could dissolve two teaspoons of borax crystals in a full kettle of water and boil for fifteen minutes, topping up with water as necessary. In all these cases make sure that you rinse out the kettle thoroughly and wipe out any remaining loose lime scale in the morning before you use it.

Milk pans

You will find that milk saucepans are much easier to clean if, immediately after use, they are turned upside down and left to stand on the draining board for a few minutes before washing.

Chopping board

It is a very good idea to keep three separate chopping boards; one for onions, garlic and chillies, one for raw meats and fish, and one for everything else. This way, when you are preparing a meal, you don't need to worry about cleaning your board every time you need to chop a new ingredient.

If however, your chopping board has become smelly because you have been cutting foods such as onions, garlic or fish, rub the board thoroughly with half a cut lemon. The acid in the lemon will neutralise the strong odours lingering on the board.

Freezer efficiency

A freezer will always run more efficiently when it is full. If you have any spaces in your freezer these should be filled with plastic bottles three quarters full of water. When you need to remove these bottles to make room for your food, you will have ice-cold drinking water on hand as the ice in the bottles melts.

Drinking water

How long do you wait for the tap to run cold before filling your glass with water? To conserve water, clean out some empty glass bottles, fill them with tap water and store in your fridge. This way you will always have cold bottled water to hand.

Quick tip

WOODEN SPOONS

Wooden spoons can quickly become discoloured and grubby in appearance. To freshen and clean them up, soak them overnight in a pint jug of water with three tablespoons of lemon juice added.

Unblocking a sink

If all your efforts to unblock the kitchen sink have failed, before calling out a plumber, try crumbling three Alka-Seltzer indigestion tablets into the plug hole and then pouring down a cup of white vinegar. Wait for a few minutes and then pour a kettle full of boiling water down the plug hole and you should find that your sink will now be clear.

"I got the blues
thinking of the future,
so I left off and made
some marmalade.
It's amazing how
it cheers one up to
shred oranges and
scrub the floor."

D.H. Lawrence

Masking cooking smells

To remove the lingering smells after you have cooked and eaten a meal, heat some fresh orange or lemon peel in the oven (180°C/350°F/gas mark 4) for 10 to 15 minutes. Your kitchen aroma will then be replaced with a fresh citrus scent. A few vanilla pods left in an open jar will also help.

Refrigerator odours

To eliminate unpleasant or overpowering odours in the refrigerator always cover smelly foods with cling film, or store in a sealed container. Then place a small bowl of bicarbonate of soda in the fridge to help absorb any remaining smells. Change the bicarbonate of soda whenever you notice your fridge is becoming smelly again.

Keeping a piece of charcoal in your refrigerator will also absorb any strong odours and keep the interior smelling sweet. Remember to replace the piece of charcoal every five to six months, or sooner for very strong odours.

A small pad of cotton wool soaked in vanilla essence is a good 'quick fix' to keep your fridge smelling sweet, but it will only mask an odour in the short term, not remove it.

Dry and fresh rubber gloves

After using rubber gloves you should always let them air dry naturally by turning them inside out and hanging them up. Don't be tempted to dry them over a heat source. When they are dry turn them the right way round and sprinkle fragrant talc inside. Next time you come to use them they will slide on easily and will smell fresh.

Spilled egg

Trying to clear up a broken raw egg from the kitchen floor can be a frustrating and messy experience. Make the job a lot easier by sprinkling table salt liberally over the gooey mess. After a few moments you will see that the salt has caused the egg white to coagulate, enabling you to clear it up more easily. I tend to scoop up the salted egg with my dustpan, which prevents me from dropping bits between the spillage and the bin.

Easy fold plastic bags

Fold plastic bags over a turned-on TV screen or computer monitor and the static electricity produced will enable them to remain perfectly flat, making them easier to fold. This way, you can store your plastic bags more efficiently as they take up much less space.

Quick tip

FLOURY HANDS

You can virtually guarantee that the phone will ring when you are baking and as soon as your hands are covered in grease and flour. Before you prepare to cook, make sure you have a plastic bag nearby to pop over your hands quickly to avoid either a very messy phone, or a missed call.

Burnt oven trays

To remove nasty hardened on burn marks from your oven trays, sprinkle the burnt areas with bicarbonate of soda and moisten slightly with water. Leave the tray to stand overnight then rinse thoroughly in warm water. The worst of the burnt bits will wash away, but if you have any stubborn marks, try scrunching up a sheet of silver foil and using this to remove the remainder.

Burnt pans

If you have burnt the bottom of your saucepan, then pour a can of cola into the pan and bring it to the boil (watch it carefully!) then allow it to simmer for about 10 minutes. When you tip out the cola the burnt on food will wipe away easily.

Alternatively you could try simmering some onion skins in a little water, in the affected pan for an hour, making sure that it does not boil dry during this time. Leave it to cool overnight and the blackened residues should easily clean off the following morning.

Fat spills

If you spill hot fat onto the kitchen work surface, or especially onto the floor, then immediately pour cold water gently over the fat to make it more visible and therefore much safer. It also helps the fat to solidify, which makes it easier to clean up. Afterwards wash the area with hot soapy water.

Oven doors

As part of your everyday cleaning routine, try to get into the habit of wiping your oven door and hob with white vinegar. Not only does it cut through grease and grime well, but it will also leave the surface nice and shiny.

FRESH KITCHEN

If you are going away for a few days a simple way of ensuring that you return to a fresher smelling kitchen is to leave a lemon cut into slices in an open dish.

Efficient grilling

My mum always used to line her grill pan with a layer of aluminium cooking foil. Her reason was that the foil collected any drips of fat and prevented food from becoming burnt on to the base of the pan. She would wait until the fat cooled and then gather up the foil and throw it in the bin. There is, however, another benefit to lining your grill pan with foil; it increases the efficiency of your grill, therefore saving energy.

Freezer power cut

If there is a power cut, remember not to open the freezer door. If the freezer is left undisturbed, the food will remain frozen for up to 24 hours, but once the door has been opened the defrosting process will be greatly accelerated.

My idea of housework is to sweep the room with a glance.

Anon

Bathroom

chapter 2
Bathroom

This room comes second only to the kitchen for wear and tear. But that doesn't mean that you have to break your back every time you clean the bath, or struggle to keep that shower grout clean and white. Use the following tips and you will find that cleaning your bathroom will no longer be a dreaded chore, but something you can actually enjoy doing.

Bathroom odours

A quick way of masking an unpleasant odour in the bathroom is to light and extinguish a couple of matches. The aroma of the smoking match will linger and temporarily mask the smell. As a considerate host you should be ready to use this trick when you have guests who might use the bathroom in close succession — particularly following spicy food!

Quick tip

FLAPPING SHOWER CURTAIN

To prevent a shower curtain from flapping around you when you shower, sew some lead fishing weights or even small coins into a hem at the bottom. Remember not to use anything with iron content or else the steam will cause them to rust which will stain the curtain fabric.

Towel care

New towels often shed fluff for the first couple of washes so wash them on their own to avoid all your other garments becoming covered. Remember also that using fabric conditioner when washing towels will gradually erode their absorbency, so use it sparingly if you have to use it at all.

Soapy sponge

A great ready-soaped sponge can be made by cutting a slit into the side of a large bath sponge and slipping in any leftover pieces of soap. This is a good way of recycling those bits of soap you would normally throw away and also ensures the kids always use soap in the bath.

Lost toothpaste cap

If the top of a tube of toothpaste goes missing then the paste can dry up very quickly and become difficult to use. If this happens, then either use a small amount of Blu-Tak as a temporary lid or store the tube upside down in a glass of water. Changing the water daily will prevent it from becoming stale.

Rust rings

Cans such as hairspray or shaving foam, can leave a rusty and unsightly mark on shelves, especially in a damp bathroom. If you want to stop this from happening then apply a thin coat of clear nail varnish to the bottom of the can, making sure it's completely dry before standing on the shelf. This only takes a minute, but means that water will no longer be able to penetrate the metal, therefore preventing the can from rusting.

Bathroom tiles

Off coloured or mildewed white grout between bathroom tiles can be easily restored by using canvas shoe whitening cream. Run the sponge applicator along the lines of grouting, leave for a few minutes then wipe away any excess from the surface of the tiles.

Damp towels

Try to get your family out of the habit of hanging their damp towels over the wooden banister after use, as this will cause the paint or varnish to wear more quickly. Instead, if there is a shortage of space in the bathroom, provide family members with a hook on the back of their bedroom doors and persuade them to hang their used towels on this. A major benefit to this is that they will always use their own towels, which means they will need washing less often.

Saving on liquid soap

Pump action liquid soap containers are very useful but children do have a habit of using far too much. Solve this by putting a rubber band around the base of the pump so that the plunger cannot go down as far. This will still allow them to 'pump out' plenty of the soap to clean their grubby hands, but they will not use as much and will create less mess. You will probably find that the reduced amount of delivered soap is still plenty for your hands too. Do the manufacturers deliberately make the bottle deliver more than we need in one squirt? Surely not!

Bathroom cleaning

Before you start cleaning your bathroom, first close the door and any windows and run some hot water into the bath to build up some steam. This will make the cleaning process quicker and easier as the grime and mildew is loosened in the warm, damp conditions. This works particularly well in the shower too.

SOAP DISH

A quick trick to stop the soap from sticking to its soap dish is to ensure that the dish is clean and dry and then rub a fine layer of petroleum jelly onto it. No more sticking soap.

Towel storage

If you are expecting a lot of guests, a wooden wine rack makes an attractive storage solution for clean hand towels in the bathroom. The towels can be rolled and placed in the wine bottle compartments and stored where they will be visible.

Shower mildew

If your shower cubicle is prone to mildew then keep a spray bottle in the bathroom with a solution made up of one part vinegar to five parts water. Encourage everyone in the family to give the shower tiles a quick spray with the solution after each shower. The mildew will not be able to survive or grow if this is done regularly, and it also makes your job a lot easier when cleaning time comes around.

Bathtub Rings

With four young children regularly using our bathroom, water rings around the bath became a bit of a permanent fixture. As I never seemed to have the time to clean the bath after each use, the rings built up and became difficult to remove.

I discovered this technique for removing these stubborn marks, and found that it can actually be quite easy: first you need to soak some paper towels in white vinegar and place these over the stains. Leave them in place for about an hour and then scrub with a little bicarbonate of soda.

In future, before the build-up gets too bad again, rub any marks with a wedge of lemon dipped in salt.

Alternatively, if you have a particularly bad case of unsightly grime rings around your bath, to bring it back to its former glory, fill the bath with warm water, adding two cups of biological washing power under the running tap. Leave it to soak overnight and then rinse away in the morning to reveal a lovely clean bath. Ensure that you wash the bath down thoroughly before use.

Scaled taps

Lime scale build up around the mouths or bases of taps can be effectively removed by tying a cloth or wad of kitchen towel soaked in white vinegar around the affected part of the tap. After an hour the scaling will have dissolved and the area can then be washed with warm water and polished with a duster. If the build up is very bad, you might need to reapply with a fresh cloth and repeat the process.

Temporary plug

A lump of Blu-Tak makes a perfect emergency bath or sink plug if you have mislaid the proper one.

Shower curtain cleaning

The easiest way to clean your shower curtain is to pop it in the washing machine with an old colour free towel. Put it on a hot wash with a little bleach added and it will come out sparkling clean. You do not need to dry the curtain before you hang it, but to prevent the shower curtain from developing mildew, it is a good idea to soak it for about ½ hour in a strong salt water solution before you re-hang it. If you remember to do this each time you wash the curtain, mildew will be a thing of the past.

Toilet stains

If your toilet bowl becomes stained below the water line, then pour in a whole can of cola and leave it for about an hour; when you flush the toilet, the stains will have disappeared. Alternatively, and especially for removing limescale from the toilet pan, you could drop in two denture cleaning tablets and leave them to work overnight, without flushing. The next morning the toilet should be completely clean with no scrubbing necessary.

Any water line rings in the toilet bowl can be easily removed using a paste of lemon juice and borax. Rub the paste into the stain with an old cloth (kept only for this purpose) and leave it to set. The stain should then scrub away without difficulty. Otherwise you could add three cups of white vinegar to the toilet bowl, allow it to soak for an hour, then brush and flush.

Cheap hand soap

In my house, we seem to get through hand soap as if it is going out of fashion. I have found that if I buy 'value' shampoo from the supermarket, or cheap shampoo from the market and decant it into an empty pump-action hand soap container, it does the job just as well, costs a lot less and I am not always going on at the children for using too much.

Quick tip

STRONGER SUCTION PADS
To achieve a better hold on plastic suction pads, try smearing the pads with some raw egg white which has been whisked up to a froth before fixing them to the wall. This is particularly effective in a bathroom, where the suction pads need to attach to slippery tiles.

Steamy mirrors

If you are fed up with the mirror steaming up every time you run a bath or shower try one of these two solutions. First, whenever you are filling a bath run some cold water before the hot, which will help to reduce the level of steam.

Second, when you are cleaning the bathroom mirror, use a small drop of washing up liquid on a paper towel to give the glass a final wipe over until it is free from smears. This fine coating of soap will keep the glass clear. The same can be achieved by rubbing the mirror with a little shaving foam then polishing off with a dry cloth.

You sometimes see
a woman who would
have made a Joan
of Arc in another
century and climate,
threshing herself
to pieces over all
the mean worry
of housekeeping.

Rudyard Kipling

Upstairs & downstairs

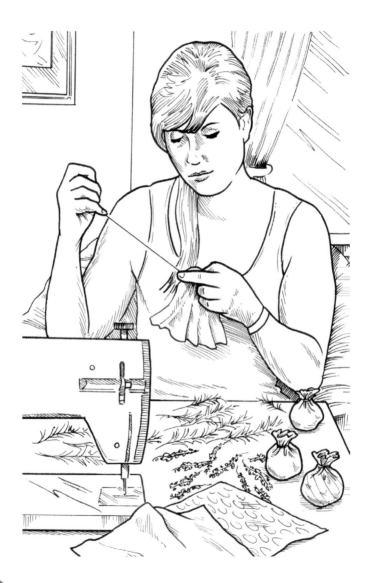

chapter 3
Upstairs & downstairs

This chapter contains lots of clever ideas for other rooms in the house, be they upstairs or down. I have included some ingenious ways to check if your pillow is still in working order, how to keep your guest bed smelling fresh, and how to stop your clothes falling from their hangers. If you never seem able to keep your airing cupboard organised then read on, this is the chapter for you.

Scented pouches

If you are about to throw away old handkerchiefs, then think about recycling them into useful, scented pouches for clothes drawers, wardrobes, and the airing cupboard. Simply place small sprigs of your favourite aromatic herbs and flowers, such as lavender and rosemary, in the centre of each handkerchief before tying the corners together with string or ribbon.

Smelly shoes

If you have the space, always store your shoes separately from your clothes. Shoes can smell and you really don't want these smells penetrating your clothes. If you don't have space to store your shoes separately, then ensure that you keep them in their original boxes with a scented tumble dryer sheet at the bottom, to keep the shoes smelling fresh. If you attach a photo of each pair of shoes to the front face of each box, you will always find your shoes in a hurry, even if they are stacked.

"A good home must be made, not bought.

Joyce Maynard

Pillow condition

Pillows will eventually reach the end of their natural, useable life. You can test to see if yours have reached this stage by placing the pillow horizontally across your forearm. If it droops badly at either end it's time to replace it.

Pillows will last longer if you protect them from the absorption of sweat, oils, perfumes, and skin creams by using two pillow cases instead of one.

Drying duvet covers

If you are in a hurry to dry your duvet covers and pillowcases and do not have (or don't want to use) a tumble dryer, then try hanging them so that they form a 'bag' by attaching only one side of the open end of the duvet to the line. This will enable the air to enter the duvet or pillowcase and circulate inside, thereby speeding up the drying process.

Quick tip

SLIPPING DUVET

To help prevent a duvet from slipping off a child's bed, simply stitch a strip of material along the bottom of the duvet and tuck this underneath the mattress. (This tip does not have to be limited to a child's duvet by the way; my husband is always accusing me of tossing and turning in bed, and indeed when I wake up the duvet is rarely where it started!)

Wake up call

If you are one of those people who really has trouble waking up in the morning, despite the alarm going off, then maybe your brain has become so accustomed to this noise that in fact it has learned not to hear it. Regularly changing the ring tone on your alarm clock will help, as your brain never has time to get used to the sound, but if you are still struggling even after this then try the following. Plug the bedside light, the alarm, the radio, the TV etc. into a trailing socket plugged into an electronic timer so that everything comes on at once. It might be annoying, but it's a sure fire way of not missing that important appointment.

Quick tip

SPARE BED FRESHNESS
If you are going away on holiday or if you have a spare bed that is not used regularly, then leave a fabric conditioner sheet between the sheets to ensure a welcoming and fresh smell when the bed is next slept in. It is also a good idea to air it for a couple of hours before its next use.

Lost earrings

If you have dropped an earring or other small item on the carpet and are having trouble finding it, rather than rubbing your hand over the carpet in search of your lost treasure, bang your fist down onto the carpet repeatedly, keeping your eyes peeled, and you will find your dropped item jumps up and makes itself visible.

More airing cupboard space

Here are a few tips for increasing the available space in your airing cupboard...

- Fix a pillowcase to the back of the door, so that you can keep smaller articles handy, without them getting lost amongst the larger items.

- Screw cup hooks around the top of the cupboard so you can hang up shirts easily and without creasing them when you need to air them.

- Fix towel rails underneath the shelves on which to store your spare coat hangers, leaving you more room in your closets.

Matching sets of bed linen

If you are anything like I used to be, you will find yourself rooting through your airing cupboard to find that elusive matching pillowcase or fitted sheet, to go with the lovely duvet set you need to use. Since having four children, and having lots and lots of regular bed linen changes to make, I have found it really useful to keep my airing cupboard well organised.

After ironing (if necessary) and folding all my matching bed linen, I place the fitted sheet, flat sheet, duvet cover and pillowcases inside one of the pillowcases of the set. I then keep all my single sets in one pile, and all my double sets in another. This way, when I need to change a bed, all the linen I need is in one place.

Caring for your bed

If we are lucky we spend about a third of our lives asleep. This is why it is so important that we look after our beds and keep them in tip top condition. If you can get into the habit of turning, cleaning, and airing your mattress regularly, then you will benefit from a longer lasting, fresher smelling bed.

Top mattress tips

- If your mattress smells a little bit musty and needs to be freshened up, sprinkle with some bicarbonate of soda and leave for a few hours before vacuuming off.

- To help prevent uneven wear and tear and prolong the life of your mattress, turn it regularly (about once every three months – see 'Mattress care' tip on page 51).

- Invest in mattress protectors for all the beds in your home. These do not need to be changed every time you remake your beds, but as their name suggests they will help to keep your mattress clean and they can be laundered in the same way as a fitted sheet.

- If you find yourself rolling into a dip in your bed, or you can feel bumps or springs, then it is time to ditch the old mattress and invest in a new one. Don't keep your bed beyond the manufacturer's recommended lifetime.

- Don't forget about your pillows. If your pillow is saggy, lumpy and no longer supporting your neck and head, then it's time to treat yourself to a lovely new one.

How to make a bed – the easy way

My first idea was to explain how to make a bed properly, with hospital corners and blankets, etc, etc. But I wondered how many people actually still use blankets and flat sheets? Nobody that I know. So instead, I have decided to offer up the cheat's guide to making a modern bed.
So, starting with a completely bare mattress, here goes:

- Start with a fitted mattress protector – so much easier to clean than a mattress!

- For extra comfort you could put on a fleecy undersheet – optional but cosy! Then your fitted top sheet.

- Now for the trickiest part – the duvet cover. Lay your duvet on the floor. Turn your duvet cover inside out.

- Reach inside the inside-out duvet cover and grasp the far corners – one in each hand. Whilst still holding the corners of the duvet cover take hold of the appropriate corners of the duvet on the floor and shake the duvet cover onto the duvet! Easy peasy.

- Lay this on top of your bed and fasten the poppers or buttons to secure.

- Pop a plain pillowcase on your pillow for protection and then on top of this place the pillowcase to match the duvet cover.

- Whether you keep your pillow above or below your duvet is simply a matter of taste; however, it is considered proper to ensure that the opening side of the pillowcase faces away from the door to the room.

Non-slip coat hangers

I hate opening my wardrobe door to find two or three items have fallen from their hangers and are in a crumpled heap on the floor of the closet. Simply wrap rubber bands around the ends of the hangers to prevent this from happening.

Whilst on the subject of hangers, try to use the correct size of hanger for your garment; a hanger that is too small could easily ruin an item of clothing by causing a misshapen shoulder line. Also if you must use wire hangers, always check to ensure there are no protruding metal ends that could snag your clothing.

Drawer fresheners

Instead of using expensive scented drawer sachets to make your clothes smell nice, just leave a tumble dryer fabric sheet in each of your drawers, and a few at the bottom of your wardrobe. They don't take up any room, last for ages, and are very economical.

Quick tip

LAUNDRY ODOURS

Odours that build up in your laundry basket can be eliminated by placing a couple of fabric conditioner sheets at the bottom of the basket each week.

Alternatively, instead of throwing away your empty perfume or aftershave bottles use these in the same way by putting one (with the lid removed) at the bottom of the laundry basket or in your drawers or wardrobe.

Mattress care

You can easily prevent sagging and uneven wear in your mattress by rotating it on a regular basis. Label four pieces of masking tape: Winter, Spring, Summer, and Autumn. Place 'Winter' on the top left corner of one side of the mattress and 'Summer' on the bottom right corner of the same side. Now flip the mattress over sideways and place 'Spring' on the top left corner of this side of the mattress and 'Autumn' on the bottom right corner of the same side. Make a note on your calendar to flip your mattress side-to-side and end-to-end at the start of each season and it will last a lot longer! (You know you have got it right if the correct season is stated on the top left of your mattress!)

If you find your mattress smells a little musty and needs freshening up, sprinkle with some bicarbonate of soda, leave for a couple of hours, then vacuum it off.

Top bed linen tips

- Wash, iron and store your bed linen inside out. This saves you time when replacing a duvet cover.

- Store your duvet cover, matching pillowcase, spare pillowcase, and fitted sheet altogether, folded neatly inside the pillowcase. This means that you can simply grab and go, saving time and hassle searching for matching items.

- If you are not using a bed for a while, pop a scented tumble drier sheet underneath the duvet to keep it smelling fresh.

There was no need to do housework at all. After the first four years the dirt doesn't get any worse.

Quentin Crisp

Outside, garage & gardens

chapter 4
Outside, garage & gardens

I have found this chapter the hardest to categorise, so in this section you'll find everything to do with being outside, whether it be in your garden, the garage, shed, car, or even preparation for going on holiday. If you have a leaky umbrella, cannot clean your car windscreen, or keep getting your tyre pressures wrong, then read on, the solution is here.

Wet umbrella

When you are drying a wet umbrella ensure that you leave it half open until it is completely dry. If you leave it fully open, the material might stretch and become detached from the spokes next time you close it, and if you close it while it is still wet, then it will not dry thoroughly and might become affected by mildew.

Quick tip

WATERPROOF UMBRELLA
Umbrellas are water repellent to a certain degree but rarely waterproof, as a heavy rainstorm will often reveal! A dry umbrella can be made virtually water resistant by spraying both sides with hairspray and drying completely before folding away.

Awkward umbrella

If you find that your collapsible umbrella is refusing to do just that, then try rubbing a candle or a bar of hard soap up and down the shaft a few times. Then open and close your umbrella, and the problem should have disappeared.

Travelling with confidence

It is a really good idea to photocopy all of your important travel documents (passport, insurance, itinerary etc.) before you go abroad and pack them separately from the originals. If any of your documents are lost you will still have all the information you require.

When you return from your holiday make a list of all those items that you took and did not use along with a note of those things that you wish you had taken. Put the list in your suitcase ready to make your packing more efficient next time you travel.

PASSPORT PHOTO

I have to admit to being horribly embarrassed by every passport photo ever taken of me. If you also suffer with that washed out appearance so typical of photographs taken in a booth, then try this. If you can manage it, sit with your head between your legs for a few seconds before having the photo taken. The rush of blood to your head will give you the appearance of a healthy complexion.

Holiday photos

Whenever you are travelling with your family, make sure that you take along a recent photo of everyone, especially if you do not speak the language of the country you are visiting. This way, should anybody in your party become lost, you will always be able to give a perfect description.

Suitcase smells

When you come home from holiday, and your dirty washing has made your suitcase or holdall smell musty on the return journey, place a bar of fragranced soap inside before you store it away for really fresh smelling luggage next time you use it. To help prevent this problem in the first place, remember to pack some scented tumble dryer sheets and place these amongst the dirty linen in your case on the homeward journey.

Cool box for shopping

It is always useful to keep a picnic cool box in the car boot and use it for your frozen food when you have finished shopping. If you get stuck in traffic or need to make any unintended detours you don't need to panic too much about your ice cream melting.

Frozen water bottles

To save valuable space in your cool box when you are going on a picnic, instead of using bulky freezer blocks use some small frozen bottles of water. These will not only keep the food chilled but also provide ice cold drinks as the ice in the bottles melts.

Picnic condiments

Used herb and spice jars make very useful containers for salad dressings and other condiments when going on a picnic or for 'al fresco' dining, when you would rather not have the bigger bottles on display. If you are taking a flask with you for hot drinks, the small containers which your camera films come in make perfect individual milk 'bottles'.

Barbeque pans

Cleaning the bottom of saucepans after you have used them on the barbeque can be a messy job and if you don't clean them effectively then next time you use them on your hob they will smoke and smell. If you remember to rub a bar of soap over the outside of the bottom of your pans before you use them then the black stains will wash off much more easily.

Slipping grips

After a while, the rubber grips on bicycle handlebars can become loose and slide off. To stop this from happening, paint that section of the handlebars with nail varnish remover and then put the grips back on. Don't ask me why, but this should help them to stay in place.

Rust-free rims

If the wheel rims of your bicycle have begun to go rusty this can be easily removed if you place pieces of fine grade sandpaper or emery paper between the bicycle brake blocks and turn the pedals whilst lightly applying the brakes.

Tyre pressures

I know it is vital to keep my car tyre pressures at the correct levels, but with a memory like a sieve, I could never remember the information when I needed it. An easy way of remembering what my tyre pressures are is to write them onto a small piece of masking tape and stick this to the rear of my tax disc holder on the windscreen. This saves me time trying to find the appropriate information at the garage forecourt or indeed driving my car with incorrect tyre pressures.

Quick tip

SLIPPERY STEPS

In the winter, frosty weather can cause doorsteps to become slippery and dangerous. Washing down the doorstep with a solution made up of one soluble aspirin and one tablespoon of methylated spirits to two pints of water will prevent this from happening. It is worth remembering this tip if you have a set of outdoor steps and want to make them non-slip.

Ants in the garden

One of my pet hates in the summer is when you are eating alfresco and find yourself assaulted by an army of ants, crawling up the legs of your garden table to help themselves to your food. To prevent this happening try standing the legs of your table into old cleaned out tin cans or plastic tubs filled with water. This may sound simple, but it is very effective.

Barbeque grill

There are several different ways of cleaning a barbeque grill; try them all, then you can choose your favourite:

- Rub the grill of a barbeque with a cut, raw potato before each use to help keep it clean. You will find if you do this that washing away any burnt food and fat will be a much easier job afterwards.

- To clean a barbeque grill that is already badly encrusted with food, soak it in brewed filter coffee overnight, then scrub well and wash as normal.

- Another good way of loosening any burnt on grease is to lay the barbeque grill on the lawn overnight. The dew will combine with the enzymes in the grass and make the cleaning job a whole lot easier. This also works well with dirty wire oven racks.

If you have a gas barbeque, then when you are ready to clean it turn it up to its hottest setting and put the lid down. Leave this for 5 minutes and switch off. While it is still hot, you will find that the grease and encrusted food will have softened enough to scrape the majority of it away with a spatula, before allowing it to cool enough to wash normally.

Kitchen roll holder

When you are picnicking in the garden, or enjoying a barbeque, to avoid worrying about paper napkins blowing away, put your patio table umbrella through the centre of a kitchen roll before putting the pole through the table. The kitchen roll will be easily available to everyone on the table and won't roll or blow away.

Foggy screen

Keep a (chalk free) chalkboard eraser in your car glove compartment. This cleans a misted windscreen far more effectively than any cloth.

Insect marks

If you have spent what seems like hours scrubbing away at your car windscreen trying to remove all those dead bugs after a run on the motorway, you will find this tip very useful indeed. Sprinkle a liberal amount of bicarbonate of soda onto a damp cloth and use this to clean your windscreen. You will find those stubborn marks caused by dead insects are easily removed.

Oil spills

Any oil spill in the garage or on the drive can be quickly and easily soaked up if you cover it immediately with fresh cat litter. This also acts as a marker, so nobody will walk over the spilt oil, and it can be carefully swept up later.

Oil or grease stains on a brick driveway can usually be removed by pouring cola over the stain. If this is done in the evening and left overnight, when the cola is washed off in the morning the stain should have disappeared.

Peg bag

When hanging out washing on a line, use an old shoulder bag to carry the pegs. This leaves both hands free to hang your washing, and you always have your pegs close by.

Cleaning is the best thing for the human mind and body. Seeing all the dirt being sucked up is an instant gratification!

Helena Christensen

Cleaning
& tidying

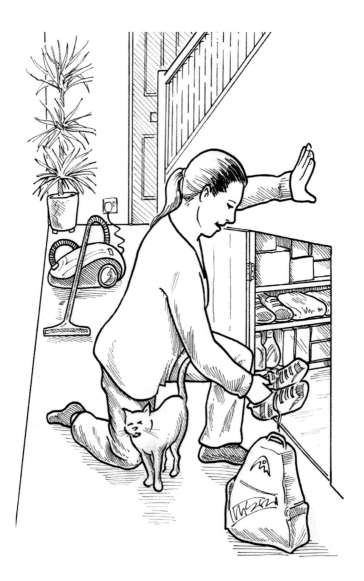

chapter 5
Cleaning & tidying

Cleaning and tidying seems to be a never-ending task, even in the absence of all the other chores that need to be done, just keeping your home in a reasonable state can be full time job. I can tidy up my house, and within 30 minutes of the children coming home from school, all my hard work is undone. In the following pages, you will find some clever ideas for keeping your home tidy for longer and some useful ways to 'cheat' at the housework. Have fun!

First impressions

Don't underestimate the power of first impressions. The most important room to keep clean and tidy is the very first room a visitor will see. If this is your hallway, then make an effort to keep this room clear of clutter and as clean and tidy as possible. Keep your children's school bags out of sight, shoes and coats neatly hung up or hidden in a cupboard.

This way, your visitor will remember this room and not necessarily your messy living room, or cluttered kitchen. It also feels much nicer, when you have been out, to come home to a room that looks beautiful. Even if it is simply the hallway.

Quick tip

DON'T BE A MAGPIE
Remember, less is more. Try to avoid those magpie tendencies. Only allow into your home those items that are useful or beautiful. Try to avoid hanging on to items which you feel might come in useful someday. If you haven't used something in a year, then chances are you will rarely (if ever) need it again.

Odd socks

To save your (or your family's) sock drawers becoming a mess, obtain some of those cardboard apple separators that supermarkets use. These fit perfectly inside a smaller drawer and will allow you to separate each pair of socks easily.
To save yourself having to root through odd socks to find a pair, keep a small bag attached to the inside of the door of your wardrobe and keep any odd socks in there for a while; as you discover new odd socks check through this bag to see if you can find their partners.

Paperwork

If you are short of space and find it difficult to keep on top of your paperwork, receipts and filing, then instead of having a separate file for each bill, invest in a January to December concertina file and simply file your receipts, statements, letters, etc. month by month. At the end of each year, simply tie a ribbon around this file and start a new one. You will always have all your paperwork neatly to hand.

Shelving and storage

Plenty of shelving and storage is the key to keeping your rooms tidy, a place for everything and everything in its place. If you are an orderly person, then open shelving can be most attractive, but remember, if you are more naturally an untidy person, then opt for cupboards and shelving with doors so that you can hide your untidiness away.

Start at the top

When you are cleaning the whole house in one go, remember to go from 'top' to 'bottom'. By starting at the top and working down you are using gravity to help, and any dislodged dust will make its way down to lower levels. Start with the cobwebs, then surfaces and windowsills, and finally move onto the floor.

There is an argument to say that vacuuming and sweeping raises dust and so should be the first job you do, but I have tried this and know that after cleaning the house, my floor always needs another go, so I would rather just do it once at the end.As you work your way around the house on a cleaning mission, take a plastic rubbish bag with you, this saves you traipsing to and from the main rubbish bin when you are emptying waste paper bins in different rooms.

Cleaning artificial plants

To successfully clean and remove the dust from artificial flowers and plants place them in a bag with a handful of salt. Tie the bag and gently shake for a few minutes. It is amazing how effective this is, and it dispenses with the need to wash them with water, or risk sucking bits off with the vacuum.

Grubby computers

Computers are renowned for attracting lots of dust and can become very dirty. This is because of the static electricity they generate, but this can be easily reduced by using a cloth dampened with white vinegar to wipe down the keyboard, the exterior of the monitor, and all the wires. The vinegar works by effectively making the surfaces 'static-proof' which stops the dust from clinging so easily.

Vacuum lead

To help the electrical lead of your vacuum cleaner rewind more easily, why not spray a little furniture polish onto a cloth (try my homemade recipe on page .....), and pull the lead through the cloth to coat the cable with a thin layer of the polish? You will find that it will now rewind much more smoothly.

Furniture moving

If you are unable to lift a piece of heavy furniture, before trying to drag it across a wooden floor, place socks over the legs of the furniture. This will help it to slide more easily and can prevent unsightly scratch marks on the floor.

Longer lasting flowers

Remember that flowers live longer in the cold. So if your house is particularly warm, try moving your flowers to a colder spot overnight and putting them back in pride of place in the morning. You might find your flowers have a longer life.

Fresh flower water

Water in a flower vase can quickly become stale and cloudy and the glass discoloured. To prevent this from happening, and to keep the flowers fresh, put a tablespoon of bleach in the water when you initially fill the vase. The water will stay clear for about a week and the flowers will last longer too.

A friend of mine used to add a little food colouring to the water in her vases, to match the colour of the flowers. This can look very effective, and it hides the cloudy water.

Safer ornaments

If you are fed up with ornaments being knocked off the windowsill every time your draw the curtains, when the cat fancies a wander, or when you are dusting, then simply stick them to the windowsill surface using a little Blu-Tak. It will hold your precious items firmly in place, without damaging your surfaces, whilst allowing you to remove them if necessary.

Quick tip

COMFORTABLE IRONING

I always used to iron standing up, until I saw a heavily pregnant friend sitting down to do hers. It takes a little practice, but as ironing can be a long and tiring business, it is well worth trying. If this really does not feel natural to you, and you prefer to stand, then why not remove your shoes and stand on a large soft cushion? This will ease the pressure on your feet and help to prevent fatigue.

The junk drawer

Every home is almost certain to have an odds and ends drawer where all sorts of small items are kept. It is a good idea to get into the habit of regularly sorting it out and filing these odds and ends into small jars or small bags with a note of exactly what's inside. Fuses, safety pins, picture hooks etc. can then easily be found in an emergency, saving time and frustration.

Room fragrance

To make your rooms smell nice, place pot-pourri into the foot end of a pair of stockings or tights, tie it up and lodge it behind the radiator; the heat from the radiator will release more fragrance. You can also use essential oils on the pot-pourri which have aromas to suit the particular room, for example you could use lavender in the bedroom, rose in the lounge, vanilla or apple in the kitchen, or lemon in the bathroom.

Another way to quickly freshen up a room is to drop a small dot of perfume on the bulb of your table lamps and the heat will disperse your favourite fragrance into the room.

Quick tip

DUSTY DOORMAT
If you put off cleaning your dusty doormat because of the clouds of dust it creates (and all that extra cleaning!) then pop it in a large dustbin liner before shaking it vigorously. Problem solved.

"Women feel happier and more in control of their lives when their home is clean and tidy. Cleaning is the new therapy.

Dee Smith

Damp dusting

Don't be tempted to use furniture polish every time you need to dust, as this can cause an unnecessary build up of polish. Instead, use my homemade polish (page 97) once a month, and in between times moisten a dusting cloth very slightly with water, and use this instead of a dry cloth. A damp cloth will ensure a more efficient job as dust will adhere to it, rather than just floating off into the room.

Remote control heaven

We seem to have an incredible number of remote controls in our house and they are always getting lost. This is extremely frustrating, because there is no way of using our DVD player without the remote. A self-adhesive Velcro tab allows you to attach the remote to the side of the appliance after use (one piece on the remote and one piece on the appliance); this way you always know where it is.

Here's one for the real couch potatoes. If you have to keep getting out of your seat because, from where you are sitting, the infra red from the remote control is not in view of the sensor on the equipment, then simply position a mirror opposite the set and direct the remote to the mirror. The signal beam will then bounce off the mirror to the sensor.

Sooty or sweep?

If you seem to be calling out the chimney sweep more often than you feel you should, a handful of salt thrown onto a brightly burning fire at least once a week will help to reduce the build up of soot in the chimney.

Handy toothbrushes

Don't throw away your old toothbrushes. Instead keep some with soft bristles and some with firmer bristles, as they make ideal cleaning tools either for the gentler jobs, like cleaning jewellery, or the more abrasive requirements like scrubbing away mould in the bathroom. They are also useful for cleaning the crevices in wire whisks, graters, garlic presses etc. I always mark these old toothbrushes by wrapping a little black tape around the handle, so that they don't find their way back into your toothbrush holder by mistake!

Named plugs

Wherever you have a lot of plugs in one place, for example behind the television or stereo, pop a sticker on the back of each plug with the name of the appliance clearly marked. This way, when you need to unplug a particular item, you don't have to go through three or four plugs before you find the right one.

Don't put off till tomorrow…

Whenever you discover a repair that needs to be made, or a light bulb that needs replacing etc., try to attend to it as soon as possible. If you do not, it will continue to bug you every time you come to use the item. Do everything you can to make it right as soon as possible to prevent the small jobs becoming bigger jobs.

Clock cleaning

An ingenious way to clean the inside of a large dusty clock without disturbing the mechanism, is to place a ball of cotton wool soaked in paraffin into the base of the clock and leave it for a few days. The dust from within the clock will be draw down onto the cotton wool which cleans the internal workings.

DUSTING SOCK

A damp sock secured to the end of a broom handle with an elastic band is perfect for removing cobwebs in inaccessible places and is so much more effective than a feather duster. The dust and webbing sticks to the damp sock instead of falling on your head.

Instant improvement

If you are short of time and can't do a complete clean of a particular room then just do a quick tidy. Open all the windows to let in some fresh air. Put away anything that is not in its rightful place, clear up any used crockery, throw away any fading or dead flowers, and empty the waste paper bin. Close the windows and if necessary give a quick spray of air freshener.

Cleaning leather

Dirty leather bags can be cleaned by rubbing them with the inside of a banana skin or, alternatively, with a cloth dipped in a little egg white that has been whisked until frothy. After cleaning, the leather should be polished up with a soft cloth.

Extension lead storage

To keep your short extension leads from becoming tangled in storage, fold the leads in half and then in half again and insert them into the cardboard centres of empty toilet or kitchen rolls.

If you have longer extension leads to store then fold them in half, feed them through the cardboard centres of empty kitchen rolls and then wrap the remaining leads around the outside of the tubes. When you get to the end simply tuck it back into the cardboard tube to keep it in place.

Animal hair

If you have pets in your home, then undoubtedly you will be up against the invasion of unsightly animal hairs on your furniture, in your carpets and even on your clothing.

Vacuuming will not necessarily remove all of the offending hair, and if you are having trouble removing pet hairs from stubborn areas, try wrapping some sticky tape around your hand (sticky side outwards) and press your hand firmly onto the material covered with hair. When you lift your hand, you will also lift away the hairs. This works on all soft furnishings and most fabrics, and ensures even deeply embedded hairs are removed.

Pet footprints

It is not a good idea to let your pets walk on your kitchen work surfaces. You might be surprised by the number of people who choose to overlook this offence by their beloved pets. However clean you believe your family pets to be, they are not able to take their shoes off when they come in from outside! It really is better not to have any footprints on your food preparation area!

"The Law of
Window Cleaning:
It's on the other side."

Anon

Walls, floors, windows & doors

chapter 6
Walls, floors, windows & doors

I remember my mother saying to me that no matter how clean and tidy your home is, if your windows are dirty then the whole house will feel dirty, and I have to say I agree. Even if my house is messy, once the windows have been polished up it seems to give the whole place a new lease of life. The same can be said for floors. When the kitchen floor has been mopped my kitchen feels clean, whether the surfaces are clear or not. This chapter will give you some hassle free ways to keep the walls, floors, windows, and doors in your home clean and in good working order.

Distinguishing damp

To determine whether a wet patch on the wall is condensation or damp, attach a piece of aluminium foil over the area and leave it for about an hour. If the problem is condensation then the foil will get wet on the side facing out – the room simply needs better ventilation. If the foil is wet on the side facing the wall then you know that the wall is damp and it's time to call in an expert.

Wooden floors

If you have a wooden floor that is looking a bit scratched and jaded then here is a great way of making it look good. Add a couple of tea bags to a jug of boiling water and then pour the contents of the jug (including the tea bags) into a bucket of warm water and use this to clean the floor. You will find the tea will not only disguise any scratches and flaws in the floor but will also help to bring out the natural warmth in the wood.

Fresher carpets

If you sprinkle a mixture of tea leaves and salt over a dull looking carpet and leave it for half an hour then brush or vacuum it off, you will notice that it seems to restore a little life back into the carpet, and the colours will appear brighter.

One potato, two potatoes...

A surprising tip worth bearing in mind is that if you have old carpets at home, then washing them with water from freshly boiled potatoes will help freshen them up. Potato water is also particularly good for cleaning mud stains off carpets, but don't forget to rinse the carpet well with clean water afterwards.

Brighter floor

My kitchen floor often looks dull after I have mopped it. If this happens, I go back over the floor using my mop and a bucket of fresh hot water, with one cup of white vinegar added to it. This works wonderfully to bring back the shine and brighten it up again.

CARPET INDENTATIONS

It can be really annoying when you rearrange the furniture and find that your heavy furniture has created what seem like permanent indentations in the carpet. There are not permanent, however, and here are a couple of neat tricks to remove them.

First just put an ice cube onto each dent in the carpet and allow it to slowly melt. As it does the water will seep into the fibres and cause them to rise up again. Once you are happy that the pile has lifted sufficiently, gently blot the carpet with a dry cloth and use a stiff brush to encourage the fibres to lift up again.

Alternatively hold a steaming iron just above the dented carpet and force the steam into the carpet pile using the 'extra steam' button on the iron. (Be very careful not to allow the iron to touch the carpet, though.) The fibres should spring back into place very quickly.

Carpet sweeper

It is well worth investing in a carpet sweeper. I have a wonderful sweeper that cost me less than £20 and I have found that it often saves me vacuuming as I am more likely to sweep up just a small area. When I am in a hurry to clean up, I will reach for my sweeper as it's just as effective and takes much less effort; it is also much quieter, so people watching television don't shout at me.

Carpets

Unless you have a very good vacuum cleaner, with an integral brush, the suction is often not enough to really bring up the pile on your carpets. To give them a really thorough clean, before vacuuming, first use a stiff bristled house-broom, and sweep the carpet against the pile. This needs a little effort, but it will help to dislodge the dust and dirt. After sweeping, vacuum thoroughly and your carpets will look fresh and clean, and the pile will be completely rejuvenated.

Curtain cleaning

Cleaning your own curtains at home can be a risky business as a lined curtain is made up of more than one type of fabric and each may respond to washing by shrinking at different rates. Even the threads of the hems etc. might shrink, causing puckered seams. If in any doubt don't take the risk – take the curtains to the dry cleaner instead.

Scuffed lino

Ever tried in vain to remove those annoying scuff marks on your new linoleum floors, usually caused by rubber soled shoes? Well, the answer comes directly from one of my school teacher friends. She discovered it after the caretaker complained of the mop not removing the scuff marks from those black rubber pumps all the children wear. She found that they simply rub away with a large pencil eraser. (It only needs to be large so it is easy to hold, a small one will work just as well.) If the mark is too stubborn, and refuses to be erased, you could try rubbing with a few drops of baby oil on a ball of cotton wool.

Animal smells

If you find that your pets are making your carpet smell, then bicarbonate of soda could be the simple answer. Sprinkle it liberally over the smelly surfaces, let it rest for about 20 minutes and then vacuum thoroughly, and the smell will magically disappear!

Quick tip

SQUEAKY BOARDS

To stop your wooden floorboards squeaking, try sprinkling some talcum powder over the offending boards and brush it into the joints using a soft brush. This should remove all traces of noise.

Easy-peel linoleum

If you are redecorating and need to remove a linoleum floor when it is stuck fast with glue, try using a warm iron and a tea towel. Place the towel on the area to be removed and iron over this for just a few seconds. By warming the lino, you should loosen the glue underneath sufficiently to enable you to pull up the linoleum in one easy piece rather than annoying little bits.

If you have a large area to remove, then enlisting a helper to iron whilst you pull would save a great deal of time. Happy decorating!

Crystal clear windows

When I was a child, I was trying to earn some extra pocket money by doing odd jobs for my friends' parents. One mum said I could earn 50 pence if I did a good job of her patio windows. Well, bearing in mind that I was only about nine and living in Gibraltar at the time (very sunny), the windows were in a worse state by the time I had finished with them than when I started. She did pay me, but it left me with a determination to clean windows well.

Follow these tips and you will always have sparkling windows.

- **Not when the sun shines.**

  Clean your windows on a dull day. This will avoid your windows drying too quickly with smears.

- **With help from the press.**

  After you have washed your windows, and before they dry, polish the glass with crumpled newspaper. You will be amazed by the shine this gives.

- **Wear shades.**

  Wear sunglasses as you clean, and any smears will be more apparent.

- **Different strokes.**

  Use horizontal strokes on the outside and vertical strokes on the inside to help you identify where streaks or smears are.

My favourite way to clean windows is to use the same method as professional window cleaners.

1. Use a bucket of warm water with a small squeeze of washing up liquid and use a sponge to rub the windows clean.

2. Then remove with a good quality squeegee, wiping the blade clean after each stroke with a dry cloth (to avoid smears).

3. Wipe around the edges of the window frame with the same cloth and if there are any streaks wipe quickly with a little value kitchen roll.

To really dazzle your neighbours with sparkling windows, after cleaning spray them with a solution of one part tepid water and one part malt vinegar made up in a spray bottle. Then polish the windows up using a few sheets of value kitchen roll or a good quality lint free dry cloth.

Easy-glide curtain wire

Threading the curtain wire through the top of net curtains can be a tedious process as the end can often get snagged in the curtain material. Try cutting out the corner from a plastic bag and securing it over the end of the wire with a small piece of Blu-Tak before threading, and it should glide through the curtain top without snagging. Alternatively you could try doing the same with a felt tip pen lid.

Curtain hooks

When you have to take your curtains down and remove all the hooks in preparation for cleaning, remembering where the hooks belong is not always easy. Make a tiny mark with permanent marker pen at the position of each hook, and this will save time trying to decide where the hooks go when you come to re-hang the curtains.

Cleaning Venetian blinds

Venetian blinds slats can be a real nuisance to dust or clean. The very best way to dust them is to use an old woollen or cotton glove. Pop on the glove and simply run the slats of the blinds in between your fingers. Both sides of the slats will be dusted and as long as you remember to 'clap' the dust off your glove after cleaning every two or three slats so you don't end up putting dirt back onto the blind, you will find this an extremely efficient method.

Similarly, if your Venetian blinds are beyond simple dusting and are in need of a good scrub, another pair of woollen or cotton gloves will do the job nicely. (You could use an old pair of socks instead.) Make sure you have a bowl of warm soapy water close by and put one glove (or sock) on each hand. Dip one hand into the bowl of water and run the slats through the fingers of the 'wet' hand. Then dry off with the other gloved hand. Keep rinsing the wet glove in the bowl of soapy water until finished.

If you add a cup of vinegar to the soapy water, this will freshen the blinds and stop any musty smells appearing later on. It can also be beneficial to rub the slats weekly with a tumble dryer fabric softener sheet, which will help to eliminate the static electricity that builds up and attracts the dust.

Pure white net curtains

To restore your net curtains to their original dazzling white, add a couple of denture cleaning tablets to a bucket of water and leave them to soak overnight (you could use the bath, if you have a lot of nets – but add an extra tablet). In the morning rinse your brilliant white net curtains well in fresh water.

"Housework is something you do that nobody notices until you don't do it.

Anon

Non-crease nets

There really is no need to iron your net curtains. After you have washed them spin them dry and then immediately hang them back up at the window and allow them to finish drying in situ. Any remaining creases will simply drop out as they dry.

Creaking doors and stuck keys

If you have annoying creaking or squeaking door hinges then an ordinary lead pencil is all you need for a quiet life. The 'lead' in the pencil is actually graphite, a brilliant lubricant. All you need to do is rub it over all the joints in the squeaky hinges then work the door backwards and forwards a few times. Repeat this process a couple of times and soon you will find that the graphite has effectively solved the noisy problem.

As graphite is dry, there will be no infuriating drips on the carpet as can often happen when using oil or other liquid lubricants. The effect will also last a lot longer.

This graphite trick also works for newly cut keys which are tight or have a tendency to stick. Work the pencil tip over the grooves in the key and, if it's a large key hole, inside the lock as well (do this carefully – you don't want to break the tip of the pencil off inside the lock). Next work the key in and out of the lock a few times, and carefully turn the key until it turns the lock smoothly.

If the key is still sticking after doing this, then I would abandon it altogether. If this doesn't work, nothing will. Your only hope is to get another one cut from a key that you know works well.

"Nature abhors
a vacuum, and so do I.

Anne Gibbons

Silver, metals, glass & wood

chapter 7
Silver, metals, glass & wood

We all have items made of these materials in our homes, and there are many easy ways of dealing with them. I have included them within this chapter, so if you cannot clean that crystal decanter properly, or your wooden table is suffering from those everyday scratches, then use these ideas and your home will sparkle like a new pin.

Tarnish-free jewellery

My Mum always used to keep a small piece of white chalk in her jewellery box. When I asked her why, she told me that it prevents her jewellery from tarnishing if it is left unused for any length of time. This works by absorbing any moisture in the air, which is why your jewellery tarnishes in the first place. You could also use a small sachet of silica gel (often found in the packaging of electrical equipment).

Copper pans

If you have copper-bottomed pans that are looking dull or discoloured, smear tomato ketchup over the copper and leave to stand for a couple of hours. Rinse and wash in the usual way and the copper will be rejuvenated and shiny.

Tarnished silver

When my mother-in-law was a little girl (in the 1940s) it was her job to polish all the silverware in the house. She used silver polish in those days and spent a long time buffing the items up to a good shine with a cloth and plenty of elbow grease. You don't need to spend hours polishing your silver anymore – try this amazing way to remove the tarnish and be proud of your silver.

First line the bottom of your kitchen sink with aluminium foil. Then fill it with hot water and add about 50ml (1/4 cup) of table salt, rock salt, or bicarbonate of soda and stir until it has completely dissolved. Place all the silver to be cleaned in the sink and leave for two or three minutes. When you remove your silverware it will be beautifully clean! Miraculously, the tarnish is attracted onto the aluminium foil. Then give the silver a wash in warm soapy water, rinse, and dry thoroughly with a soft cloth.

Tarnished silver can also be cleaned brilliantly using toothpaste and an old soft toothbrush. This is especially good for removing tarnish from the crevices of small or intricate items. Dampen the silver and brush the toothpaste on, getting into all the nooks and crannies. Then wash in warm soapy water as above.

You will find that these methods will clean more effectively and effortlessly than most expensive silver cleaners on the market.

Scratched glass

Remove scratches on glassware, watch glasses, or mobile phone screens by polishing them up with toothpaste. The mild abrasives in the paste should blend the scratches away.

Cleaner copper

To make your copper gleam like new, try making up this wonderful recipe for copper polish. Mix together bicarbonate of soda with a little lemon juice to make a paste and rub it in to your copper item with a soft cloth (use a soft bristled toothbrush if you have any intricate nooks or crannies) then buff up to a brilliant shine with another soft lint free cloth. This works wonderfully to make your copper gleam like new.

Sparkling vases and decanters

If you have stains in the bottom of your narrow necked glass vases or decanters and find them difficult to clean, try the following techniques to have them sparkling like new. First of all to remove any stubborn marks fill your vases or decanters with water and drop in two Alka-Seltzer tablets or one denture cleaning tablet and leave it to work overnight. The following morning, rinse them out well with fresh hot water.

Quick tip

CRYSTAL CLEAR DECANTERS

Drying the inside of a crystal decanter or narrow neck vase can be difficult and water marks can often develop if left to dry naturally. An easy way to dry the decanter or vase quickly without marks is to hold the bottom of the vessel under running hot water with the opening held away from the water. The heat will cause any water inside to evaporate leaving it perfectly dry and mark free.

Broken glass

To clear up small splinters or shards of broken glass, use a thick slice of bread and press gently over the area. Alternatively you can use several folded sheets of slightly dampened kitchen paper. Although both these methods are effective for picking up minute pieces of broken glass, larger pieces should first be removed by hand, taking care to avoid any injuries.

Misty watch

If the glass face of your wristwatch gets misted up then simply turn the watch over and wear it with the glass next to your skin for a while. The heat of your body will cause the mist inside the watch to evaporate, and your watch will once again be clear.

Quick tip

DRY JARS
After washing and drying twist-top jam jars put crumpled kitchen paper inside before storing. This will absorb any remaining moisture and prevent the lids from corroding.

Candle wax on wood

Candle wax stains on a wooden surface can be removed effectively in the following way: first of all try picking away any large areas with a fingernail, and then using a hairdryer, gently soften the remaining wax just enough to allow you to wipe it away with an absorbent cloth. Should you be left with any residue, then remove this from the wood using a solution made up of one part vinegar and ten parts water.

Home-made furniture polish

This is an old favourite recipe of mine for home made furniture polish, and much more economical than the shop-bought sprays. Mix together two cups of olive oil, one cup of water and one teaspoon of lemon juice. Pour the mixture into a spray bottle and shake well before each use. I use this spray on my furniture about once a month, but I use the same rag when I polish the furniture during the rest of the month.

Wax removal

If you are having trouble removing drips of candle wax from your candle holder or candelabra and want to make the job a little easier (especially if you use a glass one) place the holder in the freezer for an hour first. This will help the wax to chip off more easily.

Furniture scratches

Here are a couple of useful tips if you have any small scratches on your polished wooden furniture.

First try rubbing the scratches with a freshly-shelled walnut, you should find that they just disappear! Alternatively, carefully colour in the scratch with an eyebrow pencil of a matching colour. The wax in the pencil will also be good for the wood.

Heat marked wood

If a hot plate or cup has left a white scorch mark on a wooden table then try applying a teaspoonful of mayonnaise to the mark and gently rubbing it in with a soft cloth. Don't ask me why, but the mark should now have disappeared!

I hate housework.
You make the beds,
you wash the dishes
and six months later
you have to start
all over again.

Joan Rivers

Stains

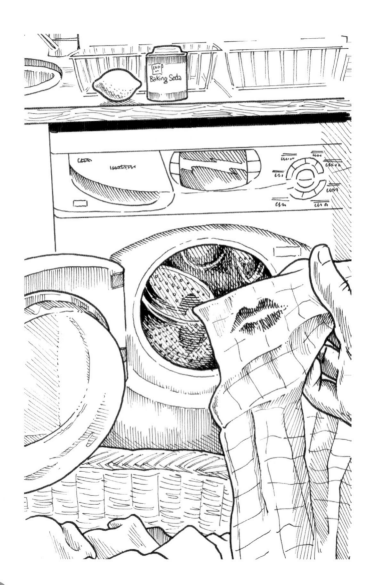

chapter 8
Stains

Stains can be one of the most frustrating household jobs to deal with. Very often, we don't notice them until it is too late, and I have thrown out more items of clothing because of a bad stain than for any other reason. Hopefully I have included enough ideas in this chapter to help you treat the majority of stains (and most of them with ingredients you will already have in your home) without the need for expensive stain treatments.

Treating stains

When you are attempting to treat a stain, always remember to work from the outside of the stain and move towards the middle. If you start at the centre and work your way to the edges, or just try rubbing up and down, you might only succeed in spreading the problem further.

Lipstick

There are a few different methods you can try to remove lipstick stains. On your best dining napkins, rub the stain gently with a little petroleum jelly or eucalyptus oil, working inwards from the outside, taking care not to spread the stain. Then launder on a hot wash cycle with biological washing powder.

On other material or clothing try sponging the lipstick mark with a paste made up of bicarbonate of soda and lemon juice. Then wash it as normal and this should remove the stain completely.

Soot

Never try rubbing to remove a soot stain from any fabric and don't wet it either as this will just result in smearing the stain and pushing it further into the fabric. Simply cover the area with salt and use a stiff brush. If you have a soot stain on a very delicate fabric which will not endure a stiff brush, try wrapping a little masking tape around your hand, sticky side out and use this to 'blot' away the soot. Remember to move the tape around so that you are not placing the soot back onto your fabric.

Pollen

In the same way as for soot stains (see above tip) don't allow the pollen to get wet or attempt to rub it off. Simply use the tape trick and pull the pollen off the fabric.

Sweat

Sweat can be a very difficult stain to remove as it is made up of some of our body's most powerful pheromones and nature means it to stay put! Try one of these two methods:

- Sponge the stain with white wine vinegar, rinse and then wash on the hottest cycle safe for the particular material, using a biological washing powder or liquid.

- Alternatively you could crush three aspirins into a little warm water and add some cream of tartar to make a paste. Rub the paste into the sweat stain and leave to work for about 20 minutes before rinsing off and washing as normal.

Shoe polish

If you have marked a carpet with shoe polish (which often happens if you have not thoroughly removed the polish from your shoes), or have some shoe polish marks on your clothing, try this tip to aid removal. Apply a waterless mechanic's soap or gel (available at DIY stores or car accessory shops) to the stain and work from the outside towards the centre with a clean cloth and then leave for 30 minutes. Wash away the soap or gel and if any marks remain then finish off by scrubbing with washing up liquid.

Vomit

Vomit! This really is one of the most unpleasant stains to remove. If you have ever tried to clean it up using normal cleaning solutions or bleach you have probably found that the unpleasant aroma returns in a few days!

If you follow this two-stage process, then you will be able to eliminate the nasty odour for good. Before even trying to remove any solids, liberally sprinkle the area with white vinegar. This will neutralise the acids in the vomit and it will also drive away the smell. Then scrape away the solids (an old dustpan works wonders for this job). Then sponge some more white vinegar onto the remainder before cleaning as normal to get rid of the actual stain and any germs.

Rust spots

All traces of rust on kitchen utensils can be easily removed using a wine cork dipped in olive oil.

Stain removal toolbox

- Petroleum Jelly
- Eucalyptus Oil
- Bicarbonate of Soda
- Lemon Juice
- Sellotape
- White Wine Vinegar
- White Vinegar
- Aspirin
- Cream of Tartar
- Olive Oil
- Fresh Pear
- Methylated Spirits
- Salt
- Sugar
- White Wine
- Newspaper
- Wine Cork
- Talcum Powder
- Baby Oil
- Denture Cleaning Tablets
- Toothpaste
- Shampoo
- Cornstarch
- Hairspray

Mascara

I was putting on my make up in the car (and no, I wasn't driving at the time); whilst struggling to put the wand back in the tube, I dropped it onto my lap. Lovely! I tried washing the material by hand, but it just smudged and made it worse. Someone told me to try rubbing the stain liberally with petroleum jelly and leaving it to set for about half an hour, then to rinse it with soapy water and wash as normal. That's one skirt saved.

If you favour waterproof mascara, try using methylated spirits in the same way, but just leave for a few minutes before rinsing and washing as above.

Salt

Salt has a natural abrasive quality which makes it the perfect ingredient for removing burn marks from dishes, and stains on crockery and cutlery. For example, those annoying black marks on your cutlery (caused by eggs) can be removed if you pop some salt on a damp cloth and rub the marks gently away. Burn marks can be tackled in the same way.

Tea

I have lost more tablecloths to tea spills than to any other stains, but since I have discovered this tip, I haven't thrown away a single tablecloth. So when you are pouring tea, if you spill or drip any onto the tablecloth, then immediately sprinkle some sugar onto the spillage. I'm not sure exactly how it works, but if you wash the tablecloth in your usual way, you will find the tea has left no lasting mark. This tip works just as well if you spill some tea onto your clothes.

Beetroot

Beetroot stains can be effectively removed from fabrics if you cut a pear in half and rub the cut face of it over the stain, and then wash as usual.

Candle wax

My son can get a little enthusiastic at birthday time. It doesn't even have to be his birthday! As long as there are candles to blow out, he is content. The only problem is that he blows candles out with the power of a force 9 gale. The result is candle wax everywhere – walls, chairs, tables, and carpets.

Candle wax is fairly kind to most surfaces, and can usually be picked or scraped off with a fingernail once it has dried. However, it is not so easy with carpets, as the wax drips down between the fibres and glues them all together. There is a simple solution though.

To remove candle wax from your carpet (or any other fabrics) cover the affected spot with a brown paper bag or a piece of brown paper and run across the top of this with a hot iron. The heat will melt the wax which is then absorbed into the brown paper. Keep moving the bag or paper so you are ironing on a clean part until all of the wax has been removed into the paper. Remember to change the paper regularly if you need to remove large areas of wax so that you don't iron old wax back into the carpet. This technique won't do your iron any harm, and it is worth bearing in mind that it even works with old, dried up wax.

"Cleaning your house
while your kids
are growing up is
like clearing the
pavement before
it stops snowing.

Phyllis Diller

Grass

Grass stains on clothes (and indeed many other stubborn marks) can be removed by using this simple method. First spray the item with pure lemon juice and then hang it in direct sunlight before washing as normal. This will work on both white and coloured clothes and will not discolour the material.

Grease

If you are left with a greasy food stain on a delicate or non-washable material after a night out, before rushing off to the dry cleaner, try this tip. First sprinkle the affected area with talcum powder then leave for five minutes before brushing off with a soft cloth. Should any of the mark remain, this can be treated with dry cleaning fluid, which can be obtained from your local dry cleaner.

Alternatively, you could sandwich the stained part of the fabric between two pieces of brown paper and press it firmly with a hot iron. The grease will be melted by the iron and soaked up by the brown paper.

Crayon

I was merrily chatting away to a friend on the telephone whilst watching my delightful children playing beautifully together. It took a few minutes before I realised with horror that I was watching them crayon all over the living room walls. As you can imagine, this tip came in very useful here. Remove crayon stains on any hard surfaces by applying a little baby oil to an absorbent cloth and rub the crayon marks gently until they disappear.

Oil and tar

A black oil mark or tar on clothing can be removed by dabbing the affected area with cotton wool soaked in eucalyptus oil. First of all, to ensure that you don't spread the stain, work from the outside of the mark towards the centre. For maximum effect, make sure that you change the cotton wool frequently. Then leave this for about an hour, which should be enough time for the eucalyptus oil to break down the stain. The residue can then be completely removed by scrubbing the area with soap and water.

Tomato Ketchup

To remove a tomato ketchup stain (or in fact any pickle or sauce stain) from material, you must act quickly. For washable fabrics first remove as much of the excess as possible, then rinse under running cold water, from the reverse of the material if feasible, to force the stain out. Then sponge the area with warm water and washing up liquid. If any residue remains, as can happen with strong sauces, then dab the area carefully with methylated spirits. Finally wash the garment as normal.

If you have a sauce stain on furniture fabric or a carpet, remove as much of the excess as possible and try to sponge well with upholstery shampoo, then rinse with clean water.

For non-washable items, again remove as much of the excess sauce as possible but gently sponge with just cold water then blot with kitchen roll or a clean dry cloth. If the stain persists then a visit to the dry cleaner is called for!

Ink

The removal of an ink stain on a white shirt can be made easier by rubbing white toothpaste into the stain using a toothbrush or nailbrush. Leave this for just a few minutes, rinse the garment and you should find that, after washing, the stain has completely gone.

Grubby collars

Dirty rings around the collars of shirts or blouses can be easily removed if you use the following method. Start by rubbing shampoo on the stains as if you were washing your hair, and then wash the garment as normal. Shampoo is specifically designed to remove body oils, which are most often the cause of grubby collar stains. I always keep a cheap bottle of shampoo by the washing machine as it is handy for pre-treating all kinds of oily stains in clothing. This is particularly useful to remember when you are on holiday!

Red wine stain on carpets

Should you be unlucky enough to spill red wine onto your carpet, then immediately pour enough (cheap) white wine, lemonade or soda water to cover the wine stain. Leave for 10-15 minutes then blot it out and repeat if necessary. Ensure that you give the affected area of the carpet a good shampoo afterwards, even if the stain appears to have gone, as the sugars in the wine, lemonade, or soda will cause dirt to stick to the carpet, and you will be left with another dirty mark.

Red wine stain on fabrics

Soak a fresh red wine stain with a glass of (cheap) white wine to keep it from setting, or cover the area with salt and then soak in cold water. Spot treat with liquid detergent before washing as normal. Alternatively spray or pour a liberal amount of soda water or lemonade onto the stain. This will dilute and neutralise the red wine. Leave the soda water or lemonade soaking into the stain for 10-15 minutes then rinse it out and wash the garment as normal.

Blood stain on carpets

Removing blood stains from carpets and furniture can be tricky but is by no means impossible. If you are lucky enough to catch the stain immediately, the majority of fresh, wet blood can be removed by sprinkling the affected area with cornstarch. This will absorb the blood which can then be carefully brushed off. It is important to re-apply the cornstarch as often as necessary until no liquid blood remains. For any residue that remains, or for old or dried blood stains on carpets, make up a paste of bicarbonate of soda and warm water. Generously cover the entire area of the blood stain with the paste and leave it for a while. Soon you will see the blood being drawn out of the carpet and into the paste. You then simply need to scrape off the excess paste and clean the carpet with a cloth and warm water.

Blood stain on fabrics

Fresh bloodstains on clothes should be treated immediately by plunging the garment into cold, salted water for an hour. This helps to quickly dissolve the blood's albumen. Afterwards, wash with biological washing powder or liquid.

Oil stains on silk

Removing greasy or oily stains from silk can be a nightmare. Try this tip before you head off to the dry cleaner. First place a clean, dry, absorbent cloth underneath the stain, then sprinkle baby powder liberally on top. Rub the powder into the stain gently with your finger, then take another clean absorbent cloth and rub the baby powder off. You should find the stain has completely gone. Don't ask me how it works — it just does!

Tea and coffee on china

Don't be tempted to bleach out the inside of your cups, mugs or teapots to remove stubborn tea and coffee stains, as bleach is very harsh and can harm the inside of your chinaware. Try these, more gentle, methods instead:

Fill the affected mugs, etc. with hot water and add one or two denture cleaning tablets (depending upon size). Leave these overnight and rinse well the following morning and you will find that all the stains have disappeared. This works particularly well for stained thermos flasks too, but make sure you leave the stopper off after putting in the denture tablets.If you don't have any denture tablets to hand, then try using a teaspoon of washing powder and fill your vessels with boiling water. After the water has cooled, rinse and clean as usual.

Plastic food container stains

Plastic food containers regularly used in the fridge or freezer can sometimes pick up stains from certain foodstuffs. To avoid this happening, spray or wipe the inside of the container lightly with vegetable oil before you use it.

To remove existing stains from a plastic food container pack it tight with some crumpled newspaper and place it in the freezer overnight. The stains should have disappeared by the following morning.

Iron plate cleaner

A paste made up from an equal mixture of vinegar and salt and then heated gently in a saucepan, is very effective for removing scorch marks on your iron's sole plate. Simply use it on a cloth to rub away the offending mark. Alternatively you could try rubbing these marks with a cloth dipped in methylated spirits.

Ink on leather

Ballpoint pen marks on leather furniture can be removed with a little hairspray. Gently dab the stain with a paper towel or cotton wool sprayed with hairspray, and the alcohol in the spray will fade the ink and it will be gradually removed. It is best to try this tip on a hidden part of the leather first to make sure the alcohol in the hairspray is not so strong that it fades the leather colouring as well.

"My second favourite household chore is ironing. My first being hitting my head on the top bunk bed until I faint.

Emma Bombeck

Fabrics

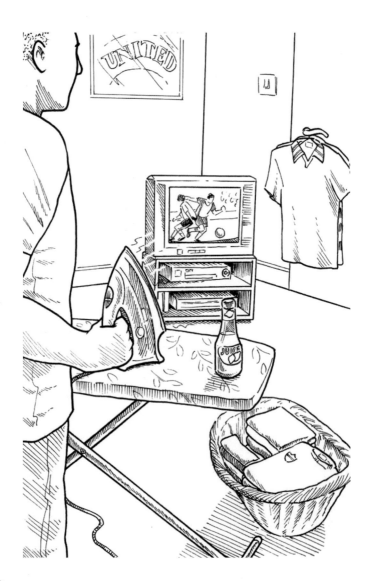

chapter 9

chapter 9
Fabrics

This chapter includes my favourite ways of making washing day less of a hassle. There are some clever ideas for reducing your ironing load, preventing your colours from running, or restoring that jumper which you have just shrunk in the wash! Also included are some tips to help you prolong the life of the more difficult items to clean!

Water marks

If your water is leaving marks on your clothes this means that you are likely to have hard water. The hardness of water causes it to interfere with the effectiveness of detergent and leaves a film on the clothing. To remove this film, try soaking the clothes in a mixture of one gallon of water and one cup of vinegar. To prevent this from happening in the future, you can add a water conditioning product along with the detergent, or add a cup of borax. This will soften the water and freshen the wash at the same time.

Baseball caps

Trying to wash a grimy baseball cap can easily destroy its shape. If, however, you simply put it in the top rack of the dishwasher and run on a hot cycle (with the dishes if you like!) it will emerge clean and fresh ready to be hung by the peak on the line to dry.

Quick tip

DRYING TROUSERS

If you detest ironing, then hang your trousers on the line by the ankle end. The weight of the waistband will pull out the majority of creases in the trousers, so you are effectively using gravity to help you with your ironing. However, if you quite enjoy ironing (yes, it's true, some people really like it!) and don't mind a few extra creases, then hang your trousers by the open waistband, as this prevents any peg marks on the ankles of your trousers.

Stored clothes

If you are washing clothes which are going into storage, ensure that you do not use fabric conditioner on the final wash. Fabric conditioner has been shown to accelerate mould growth on clothes that are packed away for a length of time.

Delicate creases

Delicate fabrics such as silk or velvet can be a nightmare to iron because of the added worry of scorching the fabric or making it shiny. Solve this problem by simply hanging this type of garment on a good quality coat hanger in a steamy bathroom. You will find that the creases will fall out without any ironing at all.

Fluff on clothes

When washing dark coloured clothes prevent them from picking up fluff by turning them inside out first.

Preserving pleats

To ensure that pleated skirts retain their perfect pleats after washing, hang them out to dry by the waistband with clothes pegs clipped to the bottom of the pleats to hold them in place. This cuts down your ironing time.

Chewing gum

Chewing gum stuck to clothing, furniture or carpets can be a nightmare to remove. If you are unlucky enough to get some stuck to clothing or fabric, put the item in the freezer (if it is small enough) and wait for the chewing gum to freeze, then you scrape it off with a knife. If there is any left on the fabric, it can be scrubbed off carefully using white vinegar. If you have chewing gum stuck to carpet or an item that is too large to put in the freezer, then placing an ice cube on top of it should harden it enough to remove it in the same way.

Hard water

If you live in a hard water area, you might find over a period of time that your coloured clothes can appear dull. A quick and ingenious remedy is to simply add a teaspoon of table or cooking salt to your washing powder. Amazingly you will find that the colour of your clothes will be rejuvenated.

Cleaning Velcro

If you have shoes or clothes with Velcro fastenings and they have become so clogged up that you are unable to use them, give them a new lease of life by using a wire suede brush to remove the built-up fluff.

> "You can't get spoiled if you do your own ironing.

Meryl Streep

Old net curtains

If you have an old net curtain, cut and sew up sections of it to make useful laundry bags for your washing and drying. Delicate clothes can be washed separately in a bag, to prevent them from getting snagged by zips etc. on other garments, and socks and underwear can be separated into different bags to avoid them getting mixed up in the wash. This is especially useful for families with young children, as it saves valuable time spent sorting socks, and these laundry bags can be invaluable when teddy needs a wash!

Ironing sleeves

If you need to iron a jacket, but do not want to create a crease mark along the sleeve, then roll up a thick magazine and push this into the sleeve. The magazine will immediately unroll and make a firm pad which will allow you to iron the sleeve, without creating a creased edge.

Quick tip

IRONING

When you are ironing your family's clothes, sort them into piles as you go, so that each pile of freshly ironed clothes can be taken directly to the correct family members wardrobe, and quickly put away, rather than having to sort everything later.

Avoiding colour-run

When washing multi-coloured clothes, one tablespoon of salt added to the washing powder will help prevent any of the colours from running into the white areas. This is also a useful tip to remember if you are on holiday and only have a small amount of clothing to wash. Rather than paying for two or three very small washes, you can pop them all in the same wash.

Discoloured underwear

Over a period of time white underwear can become slightly grey and dull. To help bring the whiteness back, place the underwear in a saucepan of water, along with a few slices of lemon. Bring the water to the boil and keep it bubbling for about ten minutes, whilst stirring with a wooden spoon. Remove the clothes and allow to cool and dry.

Iron water drips

When using a steam iron you can sometimes get water drips from the base of the iron, causing those annoying water marks on the fabric. To avoid this from happening, after filling the reservoir with water, ensure you wait until the iron has reached the pre-set temperature before ironing.

Drying woollens

When line drying woollens you can end up with small stretched sections where the clothes pegs have been. To avoid this, thread a pair of tights, a stocking or even a bra through the sleeves of the garment and peg to the line by the ends of the nylon and not the woollen item.

How to iron a shirt

- Start with the collar – iron from tips towards the centre.

- Flatten the shoulder section over the pointed end of ironing board and also work from outside in towards the centre, ironing one side and then the other.

- Turn your attention towards the cuffs now; if you have button cuffs then you can simply iron flat. If your shirt needs cufflinks then iron back of cuffs, then fold to appropriate fixing and iron in a good sharp crease.

- Now iron the sleeves, back and front.

- Using the pointed end of the ironing board again, fit your shirt onto it to allow you to iron the top part of the front panel. Then continue until the entire front panel is finished.

- Move over to the other side of the shirt and repeat.

- Iron back of the shirt. Voila!

Things to remember

- Ensure your iron is at the correct temperature for the fabric of your shirt.

- If your shirt is cotton or linen, for that extra sharp finish, use a spray bottle filled with water to moisten the surface of the fabric before ironing.

- Do not fold the collar of your business shirts down until you are about to wear them. Keep the collars facing upwards as this prevents them from becoming flattened on their hangers.

Frost free washing

If it is a cold day and you still want to hang your washing on the line, but are worried about the temperature dropping and the whole lot freezing, then fear not! A little table salt added to the final rinse will ensure that the clothes will not end up like pieces of cardboard on the line, as it prevents the water in the damp garments from freezing.

Hem creases

If you need to let down the hem of a pair of trousers or a skirt and the original creases are visible, try rubbing a bar of soap over the inside of the crease and then iron over the front of the material with a hot steam iron. (Protect with a cloth if necessary.)

Another method is to sponge the creases with white vinegar and then place a damp cloth over the item and with the iron on a warm setting, iron the creases out.

Fresher ironing

Clothes that have been stored for a long time in the wardrobe can smell a little musty when you come to iron them. If you add a few drops of lemon juice, lavender oil or fabric conditioner to the water reservoir in your iron and steam the clothes often as you iron, your clothes will soon have lost that musty smell, and not only will you have freshened up your clothes, you will have freshened up your room as well!

Adding a few drops of your favourite perfume or aftershave to the water reservoir when you are ironing for a special occasion, will make your clothes smell wonderful for the whole evening.

PEG MARKS

To avoid peg marks on your clothes when you hang them on the line, try to position the pegs in places where the resulting marks will not be seen, as often these marks will not iron out. For example, waistbands, sock toes, under arms.

Efficient ironing

I don't hate ironing, really I don't. I just hate the fact that it takes me away from getting on with the rest of my life. If, like me, you think life is too short to spend it slaving over the ironing, try lining your ironing-board, underneath the fabric cover, with aluminium baking foil. The heat from the iron is then reflected back causing the stubborn creases to be removed more easily, therefore shortening your ironing time.

Fresh laundry

To give your laundry that 'just off the line' smell, place one or two unwrapped bars of your favourite fragranced soap between the layers of towels and bedding in the airing cupboard. You could also use tumble dryer fabric sheets, although these do not last quite as long.

I find this tip particularly useful when I am storing laundry or clothing that might not be used for a while.

Rescuing shrunk woollens

If you have ever been unlucky enough to shrink a woollen item in the wash, then you will know how difficult it can be to restore it to its former glory. You could try the following tip before offering your garment to a smaller member of the family!

First of all, wash the affected item in a mixture of hair conditioner and warm water. Then reshape the garment by pulling gently whilst it is still wet. Lay it flat and let it air dry. Your previously ruined item, should now have regained (and retain) much of its original size. It's certainly worth a try!

Quick-dry coat

Coats can be a real hassle to dry. They seem to be hanging around the house for days before they are finally dry enough to put away. Here is a great way to speed up this process. Hang your wet coat on a strong coat hanger with a newly-filled hot water bottle suspended inside. Fasten the coat up around the water bottle and you will find the gentle heat inside the coat speeds up the drying process without damaging the material.

Slippery shoes

I often find that when I wear a new pair of shoes, the soles can be a bit smooth and I find myself slipping all over the place. It can take a while for the soles to scuff up a bit, so if this happens to you, try the following to prevent any accidents. Either rub a raw potato over the soles of your new shoes, or spray them with hairspray. Whichever method you choose, ensure that they dry before wearing.

Stronger buttons

Very often, when you purchase new clothing, you find that the buttons are not stitched on firmly enough. In a perfect world we would all over sew these loose buttons, but in reality we just don't have the time. So to prevent buttons from dropping off your new garments, carefully put a small drop of clear nail polish onto the thread at the back of the button. When the polish hardens it will be more difficult for the thread to break off.

Quick tip

STICKING ZIPS

If you have a zip that is difficult to use, to help it slide up and down more smoothly, rub a bar of soap over the teeth and work the zip gently up and down until it runs without sticking. This works with both metal and plastic zips.

Tumble dryer sponges

An alternative to using scented tumble dryer sheets is to make your own scented sponges which do the job just as well as the shop-bought sheets, and are a much more cost effective option. Take a cheap bath sponge, cut it up into squares and drop these into a container of your favourite, liquid, fabric softener. Pop on a tight fitting lid and keep it near the tumble dryer. When you are placing clothes in the dryer simply take one of the sponge pieces from the container, squeeze it out completely and add this to the clothes. At the end of the cycle they will smell wonderful! This also helps to reduce annoying static in the garments.

Reduce your ironing load

If time is precious, then don't worry about ironing tea towels, pillow cases, sheets, and other bed linen until you actually need to use them. Instead fold the items carefully and store them in neat piles in the airing cupboard after drying.
The weight and warmth generated will reduce the number of creases and therefore reduce the eventual ironing time.

Clogged iron

If the steam system on your iron has become clogged with lime scale, then fill the water reservoir with white vinegar instead of water. Steaming this through the iron over a sink should clear the blockage. Before you use the iron again, allow two cycles of water to steam through the iron to remove any traces of the vinegar.

Quick drying

If you need to tumble dry an item of clothing quickly after washing then put it in the dryer along with a couple of dry, white bath towels. The towels help by absorbing much of the moisture and therefore accelerating the drying process.

Tumble dryer sheet replacements

A face-cloth moistened with a value fabric softener makes a wonderful home-made alternative if you have run out of your usual scented tumble dryer sheets. (Maybe you have used them all in the other tips mentioned in this book!) Use your make-shift dryer sheet in exactly the same way as your old favourites.

PREVENTING STATIC

The static found on delicate or light fabrics is caused by over-drying of the material. If you pop a wet towel into the tumble dryer with these items, the air in the dryer will never get too dry as the towel will take longer to dry than the more delicate garments, thus eliminating static.

Cut tumble dryer time

Don't just transfer a bundle of washing straight from the washing machine to the tumble dryer as this will increase the drying time. If you shake each item as you take it out of the washing machine, ensuring that socks are unbundled and sleeves and collars are pulled out before placing them into the dryer, this can speed up drying time by up to ten minutes!

Longer-lasting nylons

Stretching new tights or stockings before wearing them will make them last longer. You can also prevent fine nylons from laddering by spraying them lightly with hairspray.

Another good tip to extend the life of nylons is to wash a new pair in warm water, carefully squeeze them dry in a towel, place in a plastic bag and put in them in the freezer overnight. Thaw them the next day and hang them out to dry before wearing. Don't ask me why, but it works.

I never kill insects.
If I see ants or spiders
in the room, I pick
them up and take
them outside.
Karma is everything.

Holly Valance

Pests

chapter 10
Pests

Insects and other pests around the home are definitely the most unpleasant things to deal with. Even if you are not afraid of bugs, nobody likes to walk into a room full of ants, or find spiders hiding in your bath towels. Follow the tips in this chapter to help you cope with those unwelcome visitors!

Homemade wasp trap

A simple and effective wasp trap can be made by dropping a teaspoon of jam into a dilute solution of beer in a jar or glass. Cover the vessel with paper held in place with an elastic band, and poke a hole in the middle big enough for a wasp to enter. Wasps will be lured inside by the smell and quickly become intoxicated by the fumes. They will fall into the liquid and be unable to escape. If you are eating al fresco then it is a good idea to keep these traps about five metres away from where you are sitting, and of course, out of the reach of children.

Flies and wasps

A bunch of stinging nettles grown in front of an open window or door will discourage flies and wasps from entering the house. The nettles will also attract some colourful butterflies, but do take care, as nettle stings can be very unpleasant, especially for young children.

Spiders

If you are afraid of spiders, then try this tip which was kindly given to me by my daughter's arachnaphobic school secretary. Conkers strategically placed around the house, near windows and doors will keep them away and by arranging the conkers in small bowls or dishes you can make them look quite attractive.

Woodlice

Woodlice are always attracted to the damper areas in the home so sprinkling a little talcum powder over these areas will help to deter them. If woodlice are a problem in an area where food is stored and you want to avoid the aroma of talc tainting the food, then use some baking powder instead which will have the same effect.

Insects

Make up a mixture of water with a few drops of tea tree oil added into a spray bottle, and regularly spray this around the doors and windows in your home. This will aid you in your quest for an insect-free house, as most troublesome bugs seem to detest the smell of tea tree oil. Cotton wool balls dampened with lavender essence will also discourage flies from the house.

Bin bag bother

Get into the habit of always putting meat bones and other smelly waste food into a scented nappy sack before it goes in the bin. This helps to deter unwelcome visits from foxes, cats, etc. to your bin bags. Even if you normally have no need for nappy sacks – buy some just for this tip!

Cats

If you are bothered by cats fouling in your garden and you cannot seem to deter them, then try placing fresh orange peel around the perimeter of your garden, as cats do not like the smell and might stay away.

However, if you have feline visitors who don't seem to have a sense of smell, then a harmless way of trying to shoo them away is to use a spray bottle with water in it. Whenever you see the intruder just give a quick squirt in their direction and they will think twice about visiting you again.

Mice

To prevent mice from getting into your home, garden shed or garage, block up any obvious openings with balls of steel wool as mice will not even attempt to chew through these.

Another way to deter mice, especially if you are not sure where they are coming in, is to sprinkle ground cayenne pepper or peppermint oil around the perimeter of the building and near any possible entry holes. Mice hate the smell of these products, and you can always use these inside the home too.

When laying bait in a mousetrap, remember that mice seem to prefer peanut butter, bacon, nuts or chocolate rather than the stereotypical and (probably cartoon driven) cheese! However, please bear in mind that traditional mousetraps are very cruel, and there are many different types of mousetraps on the market that allow you to simply remove the mouse to another destination.

Ants

If you are troubled with ants, try to locate their point of entry and pour a line of flour or talc to block their route, as ants will refuse to cross these substances. The same applies to chalk, so if you are unable to locate their way in, draw wide chalk lines around the edges of cupboards of shelves that the ants are attracted to. Ants are also put off by the smell of mint, so place some fresh sprigs in any areas where the ants appear.

If you are plagued by a colony of troublesome ants in your home, it can be very difficult to get rid of them without calling in pest control. You can kill as many ants as you like, but unless you get to the queen, she will just keep laying eggs, and more eggs mean more ants!

Mix one part borax crystals with one part sugar and sprinkle this mixture around the entrance to the nest. Borax is lethal to ants, but it sticks to the sugar making the ants oblivious to its presence. They feed the mix to the queen and she quickly dies. The colony will now be in complete disarray without its queen and the ants will run out of the nest, which is when you knock them off with ant powder (or a pet anteater if you want to be really environmentally friendly!). If you can't get hold of borax, then try using talcum powder and sugar in the same way, which has also been shown to be reasonably effective.

> **If ants are such busy workers, how come they find time to go to all the picnics?**

Marie Dressler

"Dusting is a good example of the futility of trying to put things right. As soon as you dust, the fact of your next dusting has already been established.

Anon

Miscellaneous

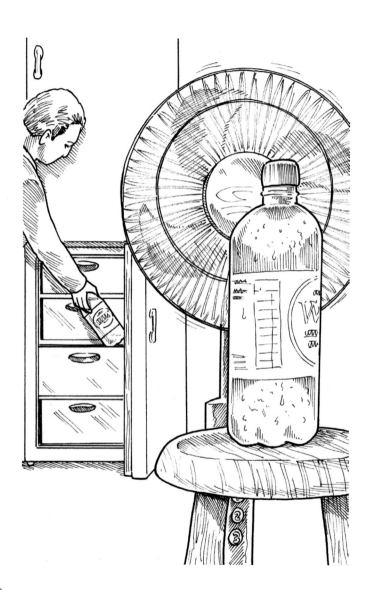

chapter 11
Miscellaneous

As the heading suggests, I have filled this chapter with all the useful, clever tips that I have gathered over the years that do not fit into any particular category. So if you lose a contact lens, find your felt tip pens keep drying out, or can't dry your children's wet wellies quickly enough – then I have the answer here.

Cheat's air conditioning

Always keep a plastic pop bottle full of water in the freezer during the summer months. This way if you need to cool down a room quickly on a hot day, put the frozen bottle in front of a fan, and it's just like air conditioning.

Smelly trainers

The problem of smelly trainers or tennis shoes can be dealt with in a couple of ways. A generous sprinkling of bicarbonate of soda into each shoe will absorb the smell overnight, and you can vacuum the bicarbonate of soda out of the shoes in the morning. For the same effect, fill the feet of a pair of tights or stockings with fresh cat litter and stuff these into the offending shoes overnight. These can be more easily removed, and can be kept and reused (depending upon how bad the odour is!).

Lost contacts

If you drop a contact lens then don't panic! It's much easier to find if you darken the room first and shine a torch around. The lost contact lens will reflect the light from the torch so watch carefully as you move the beam systematically across the floor. It is worth bearing in mind that a contact lens can land on and stick to a vertical surface too!

Picture frame

Framing a large picture can be an expensive job. To do this cheaply, have a look around your local charity shops or car boot sales. Here you will often find affordable pictures of the right size and you can just use the frame and discard the picture. Don't be afraid to be a little imaginative either, you can really bring an old frame to life with a lick of paint.

Cotton wool economy

If you use rolls of cotton wool, don't just use them straight from the packet. If you unroll it and leave it in a warm place you will find that it will fluff up to about double its original size, making your cotton wool go a lot further.

Quick tip

MEMORY JOGGER
If you have something important to remember the next day, before going to bed put a note inside one of the shoes you will wear the following morning. It's not rocket science, but it works every time.

Fire lighting fluff

It is a good idea to clean your tumble dryer filter after each use. Whenever you do this, make sure that you collect the fluff and store it in a dry place. It makes a great addition to kindling wood when you are starting an open fire.

Easy needle threading

Even with good eyesight, threading a needle can be tricky! Make the job easy by following these simple rules:

- Never break thread, always cut it with a sharp pair of scissors. This minimises the fraying which is what makes the threading difficult.

- Always thread the cotton in the direction in which it is wound around the bobbin. Thread is spun in one direction, so always go in the direction of the 'grain'.

- Don't suck the end of the cotton, as this only encourages those stray fibres to pull out.

- If all else fails, try spraying the end of the cotton with a fine layer of hairspray and leaving it to dry for a couple of minutes. This will stick together the frayed ends of the cotton.

Makeshift eraser

If the eraser on the end of your pencil has gone missing then a temporary one can be made easily by wrapping a rubber band around the end of the pencil until it fits snugly. Alternatively, a small piece of Blu-Tak can work wonders – even with coloured pencils.

Dry felt tips

If you have a felt tip pen that appears to have run out, don't throw it away just yet. Try dipping the tip in white vinegar and you will find the pen has a new lease of life.

Longer lasting markers

Marker and highlighter pens will dry out a lot slower if they are stored tip-down so that the tip is kept moist. Remember to replace the caps as soon as you have finished using this type of pens as they dry out very quickly when the caps are left off. Remember never store them tip down if you have lost the lid, or you will end up with a sticky gooey mess in your pen holder.

Droopy tulips

If you have tulips in a vase of water and the heads droop, this is because there is an air blockage in the stem caused by air bubbles in the water. This prevents the flow of water to the flower head and it flops. To release the trapped air and get the tulip head rising again, simply push a small pin in and out, right through the stem of the tulip just below the drooping head. To avoid this happening to any variety of cut flower, make sure you stand the water in a vase for about half an hour before arranging your flowers in it; allows any air bubbles to dissipate.

Scuffed shoes

If you don't have any of the correct polish and you need to smarten up a pair of shoes, then a quick and easy way to touch up scuff marks on shoes is to use a permanent felt tip pen which is the same colour as the shoe.

Keep flowers and fruit apart

If you have followed all the advice in this book regarding cut flowers, and your vases of beautiful flowers still don't last more than a few days, then take a look around the room. If you have a bowl of fruit anywhere – then you have found the culprit. The gas (ethylene), which fruits give off as they ripen, will fade cut flowers very quickly. So remember that the further away your fruit bowl is from your blooms, the longer they will last.

Quick tip

STICKING DRAWERS
Drawers that are difficult to open and close because they keep sticking, can be fixed by simply rubbing a candle along the runners. If you have wooden drawers, which do not use runners, then rubbing a candle or a bar of soap on both edges and the base of the drawer (or wherever it comes into contact with the chest) and this will help them to run much more smoothly.

Leaky washing machine

If you are unlucky enough to have a leaking rubber door seal in your automatic washing machine, then don't despair. A bicycle puncture repair kit can be used to patch small holes up very effectively. If you are unable to repair any holes immediately, but need to use your washer then turn the seal round so that the worn or punctured part is at the top, but don't leave it too long to fix, or you might end up needing a costly new one instead.

Dried flowers and herbs

I have always loved the idea of drying my own herbs, but am not very patient, and neither do I have the ideal place to hang them to dry. I have discovered a quick and easy method for drying herbs and flowers by using the microwave. Place a single layer of the herbs or flowers between two pieces of paper kitchen towel and microwave for two minutes. Leave to stand for a minute then repeat the process, microwaving for 20 seconds at a time, until the plants are dry. Depending on which flowers you choose to dry, you might find they take a little longer to dry than herbs, because of their size. Once dried, store your herbs in an airtight container.

Coffee jar castor cups

If you are worried about the feet or castors of furniture marking wooden floors or denting carpets then save the plastic lids from coffee jars and use these as protective castor cups. You might find that you have to change your brand of coffee to get a lid that matches your furniture or carpet!

Quick tip

CLOGGED HAIRBRUSH

If a hairbrush becomes clogged with hair then soak it for half an hour in a solution of warm water and conditioning shampoo. All the hair and any dirt should then easily come off the brush. It is a good idea to do this regularly to ensure that your hairbrushes are always clean.

Blocked nozzle

To unblock the nozzle of an aerosol can, drop it into a saucepan of boiling water for a few seconds (only the nozzle, not the whole can!). This should melt and remove the blockage.
Leave the nozzle to cool and dry before replacing it on the can.

Endless sticky tape

If you always seem to spend more time trying to find the end of a roll of sticky tape than actually using it, try sticking a small button on the end of the tape when you have finished with it. Next time you come to use the tape you can just move the button along and that stressful time with your fingernail will be a distant memory!

Home-made hiding place

Finding a good, safe storage place for money and small valuables in the house can be difficult. A clever trick is to spray the inside of an empty, clean mayonnaise jar with white paint. Leave the label on the jar and simply drop your precious items into the jar and store in the refrigerator.

Potato peel kindling

If you have an open fire you will know the benefit of good kindling. Keep all your potato peelings, dry them in the oven when baking and then store them in paper bags; they can be used in place of kindling wood when lighting an open fire. Just put a small bag of dry peelings in the hearth and light one corner. You will be rewarded for your efforts with a trouble free fire blazing in the hearth.

Longer-lasting coal

If you have an open coal fire, here is a very easy way to ensure that the coal you use burns brighter and lasts longer. Add two tablespoons of washing soda (sodium carbonate) to two pints of water, mix until it is completely dissolved and then sprinkle this solution over your stored coal. Make sure you allow it to dry thoroughly before using it on the fire.

Sticking plug

Sometimes electric plugs can become difficult to insert or remove from the socket. If you find that you have a sticky plug then try rubbing the metal prongs with a soft, graphite pencil and it should slide in and out much more easily.

Non-drip candles

If you can store your candles in the fridge for several hours before you need to use them, you will find that they burn for longer and will drip a lot less.

Children's rooms solutions

- Ensure you have plenty of storage — the more shelving units, storage boxes, and drawers you have, the better.

- Label each storage box, drawer, or container clearly with a picture of its contents.

- Don't be tempted to overfill toy boxes — if you have too many pieces for one box, simply use two.

- Only keep one set of toys per box, don't be tempted to allow toys to 'share' a unit, or it will become more difficult to keep organised.

- Regularly sort through your children's toys and remove any with lost or broken pieces.

- Motivate your children to clear out their toys or indeed any collection that might be getting out of hand. I find hard cash works well with my older children, and the promise of a longed for toy with my youngsters.

- Make sure your children's clothing is easily accessible to them. If they can reach their clothes easily then they can put them away!!

Things to remember

- Storage, storage, storage — if it can be hidden, then it is tidy enough! Look on the bright side, if they pile it all in the wardrobe at least you can see the floor!

- Try to remember the old rule—one toy in, one toy out—and encourage your children to find new homes for old toys they have outgrown.

I refuse to vacuum until they make one you can ride on.

Roseanne Barr

Stuck playing cards

If your new playing cards are sticking together then try rubbing the surface of them with a slice of white bread and this will make them easier to deal. Another way of getting rid of the stickiness is to brush the cards with talcum powder. This will absorb any sticky residues from greasy or sweaty fingers.

Stuck stamps

If your 'lick and stick' postage stamps have become stuck together, try placing them in the freezer for a short time. The intense cold freezes the layers of glue enabling you to gently pull the stamps apart. You could say this is a 'first class' tip!

Preserve children's art work

A quick coat of hairspray will preserve your children's wonderful artwork, and will stop any colours fading or smudging. It is also an excellent way to prevent pieces of collage work from dropping off all over the house!

Sticky labels

If you can't get an adhesive price label off something which you want to give as a gift, then simply popping it in the fridge for a while can often do the trick. This makes the label much easier to remove without leaving any sticky residue on the gift.

If, however, you do end up with that annoying, sticky residue, this can be removed by either covering the area with a little talcum powder and then wiping with a dry cloth or carefully using a little nail varnish remover on a cotton bud.

Wet wellingtons

If your wellie boots have become damp inside, then the very best way to dry them quickly is to stuff them tightly with old newspaper and leave them in a warm place. After years of trying to dry the insides of wellies with towels and balancing them upside down on top of radiators, I was amazed when my Aunt Eileen showed me how effective this easy method is.

Grubby trainers

Mud and grime, which are making your canvas shoes and trainers look dirty, can be cleaned off with carpet shampoo and an old, stiff toothbrush. Once the worst of the dirt has been removed most trainers respond perfectly well to being put in the washing machine. Pop them into an old pillowcase and wash them on their own, then allow them to dry naturally.

Perfect thanks

At birthdays and Christmas it can be a nightmare persuading the kids to write their thank you cards! A fun way of solving this problem is to simply take a picture of your children holding up each of their presents as soon as they open them. You can then have prints made to use as thank you postcards. If you have a digital camera the task is made even easier as you can quickly download the pictures and email them the same day.

MANY HANDS...
Make sure you train all the members of your family to pitch in and help with the housework. Even very young children can be given responsibility for their own items, and it might just help to prevent 'messy bedroomitis' when they become teenagers! It won't hurt for them to realise that housework can actually be quite hard work!

And one last thing .....

Remember, at the end of the day, the housework will always be there. No matter how hard you try to keep a perfect house, it is a never ending task, so don't beat yourself up if the ironing isn't done, or the skirting boards haven't been dusted. I can spend all day slaving away to make the house shine like a new pin and within 30 minutes of the children coming in from school, or my visitors arriving for lunch at the weekend – the house looks like a bomb has hit it and I wonder why I bothered.

Yes of course it is important that the kitchen is kept clean, this is the heart of the home and where you prepare your food. You need to ensure that your bathroom is clean for obvious reasons, but remember that there is more to life than a tidy house, and as long as you can keep up a reasonable level of cleanliness then you should congratulate yourself and go have some fun.

Of course, if all else fails you could always follow my favourite and most effective tip of all and hire yourself a housekeeper!

Happy dusting!

Index

'The Greatest Tips in the World' books

Baby & Toddler Tips
by Vicky Burford
ISBN 978-1-905151-70-7

Barbeque Tips
by Raymond van Rijk
ISBN 978-1-905151-68-4

Cat Tips by Joe Inglis
ISBN 978-1-905151-66-0

Cookery Tips
by Peter Osborne
ISBN 978-1-905151-64-6

Cricketing Tips
by R. Rotherham & G. Clifford
ISBN 978-1-905151-18-9

Dog Tips by Joe Inglis
ISBN 978-1-905151-67-7

Etiquette & Dining Tips
by Prof. R. Rotherham
ISBN 978-1-905151-21-9

Freelance Writing Tips
by Linda Jones
ISBN 978-1-905151-17-2

Gardening Tips
by Steve Brookes
ISBN 978-1-905151-60-8

Genealogy Tips
by M. Vincent-Northam
ISBN 978-1-905151-72-1

Golfing Tips
by John Cook
ISBN 978-1-905151-63-9

Horse & Pony Tips
by Joanne Bednall
ISBN 978-1-905151-19-6

Household Tips
by Vicky Burford
ISBN 978-1-905151-61-5

Personal Success Tips
by Brian Larcher
ISBN 978-1-905151-71-4

Podcasting Tips
by Malcolm Boyden
ISBN 978-1-905151-75-2

Property Developing Tips
by F. Morgan & P. Morgan
ISBN 978-1-905151-69-1

Retirement Tips
by Tony Rossiter
ISBN 978-1-905151-28-8

Sex Tips
by Julie Peasgood
ISBN 978-1-905151-74-5

Slimming & Healthy Living Tips
by Wendy Green
ISBN 978-1-905151-31-8

Travel Tips
by Simon Worsfold
ISBN 978-1-905151-73-8

Pet Recipe books

The Greatest Feline Feasts in the World by Joe Inglis
ISBN 978-1-905151-50-9

The Greatest Doggie Dinners in the World by Joe Inglis
ISBN 978-1-905151-51-6

'The Greatest in the World' DVDs

The Greatest in the World – Gardening Tips
presented by Steve Brookes

The Greatest in the World – Yoga Tips
presented by David Gellineau and David Robson

The Greatest in the World – Cat & Kitten Tips
presented by Joe Inglis

The Greatest in the World – Dog & Puppy Tips
presented by Joe Inglis

For more information about currently available
and forthcoming book and DVD titles please visit:

www.thegreatestintheworld.com

or write to:

The Greatest in the World Ltd
PO Box 3182
Stratford-upon-Avon
Warwickshire CV37 7XW
United Kingdom

Tel / Fax: +44(0)1789 299616
Email: info@thegreatestintheworld.com

The author

Vicky Burford is a busy young mother who manages to balance the demands of a young family whilst keeping her sanity and a relatively well-organised household! Vicky stays at home to look after her four children, all aged 9 years or younger. Prior to this Vicky worked in London as a PA. She has now embarked on a writing career and is also the author of '*The Greatest Baby & Toddler Tips in the World*'.